Rachel Coyle is a specialist property barrister who also works in commercial dispute resolution and private client. She acts in all types of commercial and property disputes, whether arising from contract, breach of duty, or otherwise. Rachel's practice also encompasses contentious trusts, wills, and probate (including TOLATA and Inheritance Act claims) and insolvency.

Rachel's expertise in property and commercial law is founded on time spent working in hedging product mis-selling, volunteering in the procurement and commercial team at Stockport Homes, paralegal work at law firms such as DWF LLP and on secondments at Hyde Housing and OneSource. In the USA, she acted pro bono in property and planning matters in the State of Virginia whilst studying for her LLM in American Legal Studies.

Clients that Rachel has worked with include global banks, U.K. solicitors' firms with domestic and/or international clients, a Cypriot law firm, start-ups, private equity sponsors, local government departments and councils, large landowners and property management companies, charities, high net worth individuals and more vulnerable members of society. As part of her private client practice, she assists and represents trustees, beneficiaries and estates with inheritance and administration-related matters.

A Practical Guide to the Housing Health and Safety Rating System (HHSRS)

A Practical Guide to the Housing Health and Safety Rating System (HHSRS)

Rachel Coyle

Barrister, Inner Temple

LLB (Hons), LLM (American Legal Studies-Draper Scholar)

Law Brief Publishing

Published 2022 by Law Brief Publishing, an imprint of Law Brief Publishing Ltd
30 The Parks
Minehead
Somerset
TA24 8BT

www.lawbriefpublishing.com

Paperback: 978-1-913715-76-2

To my darling daughter Olivia who keeps me busy and self-motivated

PREFACE

This book is designed to bring together the different definitions and understandings of housing hazards set out in the Housing Health and Rating System ('HHRS').

It is intended that this book will serve as a helpful guide of the different actions that can be taken to deal with hazards found, how to enforce notices and what other options there might be outside the Housing Act 2004 and Environmental Protection Act 1990. Whilst various legal processes, statutes and procedure/s is explained, the golden thread throughout the entire book is:

a. no one case is the same;

b. each property is different;

c. embrace a collaborative, multi-agency approach;

d. prevention is better than cure – the very purpose behind enforcement notices and assessments.

It is anticipated that the book will serve as a practical guide for local authorities, EHOs, surveyors, solicitors, tenants.

The law stated in this book is believed to be accurate as it was on 28th February 2022.

Rachel Coyle
March 2022

ACKNOWLEDGMENTS

I am grateful to my husband, Ben, for his patience and support while I wrote this book.

I am also grateful to my extended family and my clerks in Chambers for their continued support.

CONTENTS

CHAPTER ONE

PURPOSE BEHIND THE HOUSING HAZARDS RATING SYSTEM

This chapter describes what the Housing Hazards Rating System is

Purpose

The Housing Hazards Rating System ('the HHSRS') was introduced by Part 1 of the Housing Act 2004 and the Housing Health and Safety Rating System (England) Regulations 2005 (SI 2005 No 3208) which came into force on 6 April 2006.

It applies in England and Wales (Housing Health and Safety Rating System (Wales)

Regulations 2006 (SI 2006 No 1702) but does not apply in Scotland.

The HHSRS focuses on threats to health and safety. It is not concerned with quality, comfort and convenience but one's physical and mental health may be considered[1].

HHSRS does not set out minimum standards and is not a pass or fail test. It is designed to avoid potential hazards.

It encourages private and public sector landlords to review conditions regularly to ensure the property is safe and/or is made safe.

---

[1] Housing Health and Safety Rating System Operating Guidance, ODPM, February 2006, p7

It is a risk-based assessment that identifies hazards in dwellings of all types of residential premises such as HMOs, buildings including converted flats and purpose-built blocks of flats. It is designed to evaluate the hazard/s and their potential effects on the health and safety of occupants and their visitors.

The most serious hazards are called Category 1 hazards and where these exist in a dwelling, it fails to meet the statutory minimum standard for housing in England.

Overview of Enforcement

Part 1 of the Housing Act 2004 ('the 2004 Act') provides local authorities with duties and powers to tackle poor housing conditions. The 2004 Act is designed to enable local authorities to give priority to dealing with the greatest risks to health and safety in dwellings.

Although local authorities cannot take statutory enforcement action against themselves regarding their own stock, they are still expected to use the HHSRS to assess the condition of the stock and ensure dwellings meet the Decent Home Standard.

When local authority Environmental Health Officer ('EHO') inspect a dwelling, they will look for any risk of harm to an actual or potential occupier of a dwelling, which results from any deficiency that can give rise to a hazard.

The severity depends on the likelihood of that harm occurring or recurring or continuing over the forthcoming 12 months after an inspection. The factors that are considered include:

a. The age of the occupier/s;

b. Whether the dwelling is occupied by a person/s with vulnerabilities;

c. The age and/or build of the dwelling;

d. The impact and/or likelihood of a hazard/harm arising or continuing not just in the dwelling but in adjacent and/or nearby properties such as pests.

Local authorities are assisted by a HHSRS score system prescribed by the Housing Health and Safety Rating System (England) Regulations 2005 (SI 2005 No 3208) ('the 2005 Regulations').

These regulations and score system is designed to assist the local authority in determining what remedy, if anything, is required to make the property safe.

Such inspections are not isolated to only occupied dwellings. Inspections may also be carried out in respect of vacant dwellings.

An EHO may find a serious hazard (i.e one in the higher scoring bands A-C, referred to as Category 1 hazards).

An EHO may also find in addition to r instead of a Category 1 hazard/s, a Category 2 hazard/s (i.e those in scoring bands D-J) These are judged to be less serious. Action can be taken in respect of Category 2 hazards is considered necessary.

When determining what action to take, a local authority is encouraged to consider what is necessary whilst having regard for its priorities and wider policies as well as what history, if any, a landlord has with complying with notices if served.

CHAPTER TWO

INFORMAL APPROACHES

This chapter sets out the options available to local authorities outside of serving a formal notice

Collaborative approach

Local authorities must act consistently. This can be achieved by consulting neighbouring authorities in respect of areas of housing or estates that straddle local authority boundaries.

It might be that the local authority is also able to assist Registered Social Landlords ('RSLs')

who are improving their stock to make them decent and whose stock crosses local authority boundaries.

Local authorities are encouraged to comply with the Enforcement Concordat and give advice to the owner or manager on what is required to provide an opportunity to discuss the circumstances of a case before formal action.

When attempting to liaise with landlords, owners or managers, the local authority should still take into account the circumstances and views of tenants as well as. This may involve liaising with other sectors in the local authority such as social services, housing needs and housing management officers and charities or organisations that are dealing with potentially vulnerable occupants.

Such collaborative working ought to:

a. ensure that action in respect of the most serious hazards impacting health and safety is prioritised rather than have resources, scarce as they are, diverted to less serious, modest hazards;

b. ensure that occupiers are not left for long periods in unsafe dwellings;

c. secure greater compliance;

d. secure greater protection for vulnerable occupants and prioritise their needs.

This does not mean that a local authority ignores its specific duties when considering more collaborative approaches.

Decent Home

The government has committed to ensuring every social sector tenant lives in a decent home. This does not mean there is a decent home standard which is regarded as the enforcement standard but when adopting a collaborative approach, regard must be had to the same.

When considering what constitutes a decent home, this is a dwelling which:

a. Does not contain a category 1 hazard;

b. Has reasonably modern facilities and/or services;

c. Provides reasonable thermal comfort;

d. Is in a reasonable state of repair.

NRA

Regard must also be had to the overall assessment of the area including a Neighbourhood Renewal Assessment ('NRAs') and any requests for assistance by an individual such as a tenant or owner of an adjoining property, or via agencies or organisations such as the Citizens Advice Bureau ('CAB') and accredited schemes or housing forums.

The NRA consists of a series of steps that provide a method for considering alternative courses of action. The NRA is appropriate in large and small-scale assessment/s of individual properties.

Financial Assistance

Financial assistance can be provided by local authorities pursuant to the Regulatory Reform (Housing Assistance) Order 2002 (SI 2002 No.1860). What strategy is adopted is for the local authority to decide and this statutory instrument grants the local authority a general power so that optimum flexibility is achieved to desal with poor conditions in private sector housing.

Local authorities are also encouraged to consider tapping into other sources of funding, particularly when what is required to be done also improves energy efficiency and/or tackles fuel poverty.

Energy suppliers are imposed with the obligation to deliver improvements to energy efficiency by the Energy Environment Commitment ('EEC'). Grants and offers may be available and local authorities are to have regard for the existence of the same and referring occupiers/owners to apply for the same such as the Warm Front grant.

Local authorities also have the power to make a reasonable charge as a means of recovering certain expenses incurred in taking enforcement action should this be taken. This can be used as a bargaining chip when encouraging a manager or owner to remedy a hazard/s. There is no statutory limit, but the charge needs to be reasonable.

Formal or informal action?

Local authorities are more likely to consider formal enforcement important in the case of rented properties and HMOs in the private sector because this is where most of the worst housing conditions are found. The local authority may also choose not to delay in beginning formal enforcement action if there is a high risk to the health and safety of the occupant/s and/or if the landlord, owner and/or manager are intransigent and unwilling to discuss.

Where an owner, landlord or manager agrees to take the action required a local authority may choose to hang fire before serving a notice subject to a condition/s that the work/s is done within a reasonable period of time. What is reasonable is for the local authority to decide. Alternatively, the local authority may serve a hazard awareness notice so as to record the action in the event that the owner, landlord or manager do not carry out the work/s in a timely manner, if at all, and/or carry out the said works adequately.

If there is a programme of works to make stock decent, the local authority may seek to discuss the programme before the work/s is commenced so as to ensure category 1 and 2 hazards are dealt with.

CHAPTER THREE

ASSESSING HAZARDS

How to assess the hazards

Statutory Overview – Housing Act 2004 and Housing Health and Safety Rating System (England) Regulations 2005 (SI 2005 No 3208)

Section 4 provides for inspections of property by local housing authorities to determine whether category 1 or category 2 hazards exist and for the making of regulations as to how inspections of premises and assessments of hazards are to be carried out.

Amongst other provisions, by section 4(6) where an inspection has been carried out and the proper officer of the local housing authority is of the opinion that a category 1 or category 2 hazard exists on any residential premises in the authority's district the officer must without delay make a report in writing to the authority which sets out his opinion together with the facts of the case.

Section 5 imposes a duty on a local housing authority to take appropriate enforcement action where it considers a category hazard exists. Under the section the local housing authority "must take the appropriate enforcement action".

The appropriate enforcement action has to be one from the list in subsection (2). The list includes emergency remedial action under section 40 or an emergency prohibition order under section 43.

However, by subsections (3) and (4) if only one of the listed courses of action is available, it must take that course but if two or more courses of action are available the local housing authority must take whichever they consider to be the most appropriate.

Chapter 3 of the Housing Act 2004 is headed "Emergency Measures". Under section 40(1) if the local housing authority is satisfied that a category 1 hazard exists, and it is satisfied that the hazard involves an imminent risk of serious harm to the health or safety of any of the occupiers of those or any other residential premises, and no management order is in force under Chapter 1 or 2 of Part 4 in relation to the premises, emergency remedial action in respect of the hazard is a course of action available to the authority in relation to the hazard for the purposes of section 5.

Under section 43 a similar power exists to make an emergency prohibition order prohibiting any use of the premises specified in the order.

Under regulation 5 an assessor must:

a. have regard to any guidance under section 9;

b. inspect the premises with a view to preparing an accurate record of their state and condition, and

c. prepare and keep such a record in written or in electronic form. The regulations provide an extremely complicated scoring system for the assessment and categorisation of hazards: hence the use of computer programmes to assist in working them out.

Regulation 3(1) provides that a hazard is of a prescribed description for the purposes of the Housing Act 2004 where the risk of harm is associated with any of the matters or circumstances listed in Schedule 1.

Regulation 7 prescribes bands of hazards from A to J on the basis of a range of numerical scores. Thus, a Band A hazard is one with a numerical score of 5000 or more; a Band B hazard is one with a numerical score of

2000 to 4999; and a Band C hazard is one with a numerical score of 1000 to 1999.

Regulation 8 provides that a hazard falling within band A, B or C is a category 1 hazard and that a hazard falling within any other band is a category 2 hazard.

The numerical score for a hazard is reached in a number of steps prescribed by regulation 6.

Dwelling

This means accommodation that is used for human habitation, or intended or available for such use.

It includes:

a. Houses;

b. Flats;

c. Maisonettes;

d. Apartments;

e. Bedsits;

f. Hostel.

External parts of the dwelling include gardens, outbuildings, passageways, common structural elements such as rooves, walls and foundations if the dwelling is a flat, maisonette, or bedsit garages, drains, private sewers, drives and/or any other means of providing access to the dwelling.

Deficiency

This is where there is a failure that is inherent, such as a result of the original construction or manufacture, or a result of deterioration or of disrepair and a lack of maintenance. There may be more than several deficiencies contributing to the same hazard and it the cumulative affect which is significant or there may be just a single deficiency causing each hazard.

Inspection

The inspections tend to be surface and visual inspection and includes the exterior, structure and installations. Occupants are not expected to decant or move furniture and furnishings out of the way.

Exterior and structure

This is not limited to load bearing elements but includes what is essential to the appearance, stability and shape of the dwelling.

Case law has assisted in this regard such as *Quick v Taff Ely BC* [1986] QB 809, CA. The roof, eaves and fascias are within the definition of 'structure and exterior', as is drains, gutters and external pipes. The roof and eaves especially are elements of the property that give it its essential appearance, stability and shape which constitutes 'structure', see *Irvine v Moran* [1991] 24 HLR 1, QBD, at [5]. As to internal plastering and tiles, this is part of the structure, see Rimer LJ stated in *Grand v Gill* [2011] EWCA Civ 554 at [25].

The primary focus should be on what directly affects the dwelling such as the roof and windows.

Installations

The heating system is in the physical confines of the property and following Megaw LJ's comments in *Campden Hill Towers v Gardner*

[1977] QB 823, CA central heating boilers fall within the definition of installation and must be kept in repair and work properly:

> *"...the installations in the physical confines of the property must be kept in repair and capable, so far as their own structural and mechanical condition is concerned, of working properly. But no more than that."* (*per* Megaw LJ, page 835H).An installation is in proper working order if it is able to function under the conditions of supply that is reasonable to anticipate, see *O'Connor v Old Etonians Housing Association Ltd* [2002] EWCA Civ 150; [20032] CH 295.

The assessor will assess the exterior and structure of the dwelling as the inside of the dwelling.

When considering installations in particular, an assessor will look at:

a. Taps, baths, showers, hand basins, worktops, cooking facilities, food storage (personal hygiene and food safety);

b. WC basins, drains, pipes, rainwater pipes, gullies, toilets (Sanitation and drainage);

c. Airbricks, trickle vents, windows, encasements, mechanical and non-mechanical ventilation installs such as extractor fans, whole house vent systems ('WHV') (Ventilation);

d. Central heating systems, moveable heaters, district heating related installations and ducts (Space and water heating);

e. Appliances/installations necessary to ensure a supply of water, gas and/or electricity. (Water, gas and electricity).

When determining if a deficiency contributes to one or more hazards, the assessor ought to understand each element and facility including how the deficiency interferes with a function so as to create a hazard. For example, a door ought to be able not merely to open and close but also keep heat in, prevent fire spreading and be a barrier, of some sort, to sound.

When inspecting the first consideration is what deficiency/ies there is and the second consideration is whether the dwelling is capable of satisfying the basic and fundamental needs for everyday life of a household.

After considering deficiencies the assessor considers the likelihood of a member of a vulnerable group suffering a potentially harmful occurrence in the next twelve months. This is where the Representative Scale Points (see below) are used and a hazard score is determined.

Assessment

The local authority Environmental Health Officer ('EHO') is looking to see if the dwelling is 'unfit for human habitation' or 'in substantial repair'.

A 'hazard' means any risk to the health and safety of an actual or potential occupier of a dwelling which arises from a deficiency in the dwelling or in any building or land in the vicinity (section 2(1) of the Housing Act 2004). Harm can include temporary harm and health includes mental health (sections 2(4) and (5) of the Housing Act 2004).

One must look at the dwelling as a whole as well as each individual element in the dwelling. The dwelling size, type, use and build is relevant to considering what needs ought to be provided for. It is also important to consider, if occupied, the activities of the occupier/s and whether this affects the possibility of a hazard occurring or the extent of the hazard. For example, there may be damp and mould but the occupier/s failure to ventilate the dwelling when there is a means of being able to might exacerbate the excess cold, rising damp and mould.

The class of harms

There are four classes of harm:

a. Extreme – such as death, lung tumours permanent paralysis, 80% burns;

b. Severe – such as asthma, lead poisoning, mild stroke, severe fever, loss of consciousness for days, serious fractures;

c. Serious – such as chronic severe stress, allergy, serious strain or sprain injuries, sleep disturbance, stomach upset;

d. Moderate – such as occasional migraines, occasional mild pneumonia, regular coughs and colds, moderate cuts, severe bruising.

Formula, Scoring and Rating

Serious hazards are categorised as Category 1. Category 2 hazards are less serious. If there is a Category 1 hazard the local authority is under an obligation to take action. Category 2 hazards do not demand the local authority to take any action but it has the statutory power to do so.

There are different bands used when determining what category, a hazard is and the likelihood of its occurrence. A number is used to determine how likely the occurrence is as a result of hazard identified. The score is then put into a band to determine the severity.

The assessment itself is carried out by the local authority officials who:

a. Assess the likelihood of a person suffering harm as a result of any hazard;

b. Assess probable consequences of the hazard;

c. Give a numerical score using prescribed methodology;

d. Consider the numerical score against the banding and whether that banding falls within category 1 or 2.

There are three sets of figures used to generate a hazard score:

a. a weighting for each Class of Harm reflecting the degree of incapacity to the occupier/visitor resulting from the occurrence;

b. the likelihood of an occurrence involving a member of a vulnerable group, expressed as a ratio; and

c. the spread of possible harms resulting from an occurrence, expressed by percentage for each of the four Classes of Harm.

Weighting

The weighting for each class of harm is 10,000 for class 1, 1000 for class 2, 300 for class 3 and 10 for class 4.

Likelihood scale

The likelihood scale is based on the logarithmic scale of 10 to root 4. The standard ranges have been calculated by the logarithmic scale of 10 to root 8 (x 1.3335), the alternate rounded values of which give the 16 single Representative Scale Points used in the HHSRS calculation.

Lower points of the outcome scales are based on the logarithmic scale of 10 to root 3 and the upper points on the scale of 10 to root 6, and the Representative Range Points used in the HHSRS Hazard Formula are given by the logarithmic scales of 10 to root 6 (x 1.4678) and 10 to root 12 (x 1.2115) respectively, and the figures then rounded.

When considering likelihood, the assessor considers the age of the dwelling as well as the characteristics of the dwelling and the conditions found therein. When considering the occurrence involving a person in a vulnerable age group national averages are considered. Where data is available, these are given for different age groups and types of dwellings.

These averages represent the likelihood for the typical condition that could be expected in a dwelling of that particular age and type.

The assessor is not expected to give an exact likelihood ratio, but to select one of the standard HHSRS likelihood ranges. The likelihood range is of the whole dwelling.

			Representative Scale Point
Less likely than		1 in 4,200	1 in 5,600
1 in 4,200	to	1 in 2,400	3,200
2,400	to	1,300	1,800
1,300	to	750	1,000
750	to	420	560
420	to	240	320
240	to	130	180
130	to	75	100
75	to	42	56
42	to	24	32
24	to	13	18
13	to	7.5	10
7.5	to	4	6
4	to	2.5	3
2.5	to	1.5	2
More likely than		1 in 1.5	1

Spread of Harm

The assessor considers the range of outcomes under the four classes of harm. The percentage for the most likely outcome would be 100% minus the percentage sum of the representative scale points for any other outcomes.

HHSRS Standard Range of Class of Harm Outcomes			Representative Scale Point
Below		0.05%	0%
0.05%	to	0.15%	0.1%
0.15%	to	0.3%	0.2%
0.3%	to	0.7%	0.5%
0.7%	to	1.5%	1%
1.5%	to	3%	2.2%
3%	to	7%	4.6%
7%	to	15%	10%
15%	to	26%	21.5%
26%	to	38%	31.6%
Above		38%	46.4%

National average spreads of harm for each hazard can be found in data, if available, in respect of different age groups and types of dwellings.

The hazard score is thus calculated as the sum of the weightings for each class of harm which could result in a particular hazard, multiplied by the likelihood of an occurrence, and multiplied by the set of percentages showing the spread of harms.

The hazard score then falls within a Band.

a. 5,000 or more

b. 2,000 to 4,999

c. 1,000 to 1,999

d. 500 to 999

e. 200 to 499

f. 100 to 199

g. 50 to 99

h. 20 to 49

i. 10 to 19

j. 9 or less

Band A is the most dangerous and life threatening.

Band J: is the least.

The Housing Act 2004 imposes a duty on local authorities to take appropriate action in relation to hazards falling in bands A – C: these are hazards with scores of 1,000 or over.

Although not under a duty to do so, they are also able to act in relation to other hazards that are within bands D – J with a score of 999 or less.

CHAPTER FOUR

DIFFERENT HAZARDS

The hazards

There are 29 hazards set out in the Housing Health and Safety Rating System (England) Regulations 2005 (SI 2005 No 3208) in Schedule 1. These are extensive and the hazards set out include crowding and space, domestic hygiene, pests and refuse, sanitation, and other hazards.

There are four sub-groups:

a. Physiological;

b. Psychological;

c. Protection against infection;

d. Protection against accidents.

Regard must be hard to whether there is a deficiency and the impact of the same i.e does it cause a hazard/s. There can be more than one deficiency that has the effect on or which contributes to a hazard.

Fixtures and fittings belonging to an occupier do not form part of the assessment.

Physiological

<u>*Damp and Mould*</u>

This concerns threats to physical and mental health from mould and fungal growth, as well as dust mites, arising from spores which are airborne allergens. Extensive exposure can trigger allergic symptoms such as asthma, cough, eczema and wheezing. Fungal infections may arise and cause people to take treatment for cancer. The mental and social health effects cannot be understate such as anxiety and depression.

Cause: it can be caused by high humidity and dampness. This can be caused by reduced ventilation levels, increased humidity beyond 70, warmer indoor temperatures such as in the winter.

When considering likelihood of a hazard, it is important to consider:

a. that the most vulnerable group is all persons aged 14 years and over;

b. whether there is energy efficiency;

c. if there is controllable background ventilation as well as extract ventilation;

d. if there is somewhere for clothes to dry;

e. whether there is water penetration and damp proofing;

f. whether installations are installed and sealed correctly such as baths, showers, waste pipes and plumbing etc;

g. room sizes.

h. the efficiency, if at all, of rain water goods and whether guttering leaks onto the exterior of the dwelling.

Preventive measures include:

a. Damp proof courses or membranes;

b. Properly installed installations including mechanic and non-mechanic ventilators;

c. Air bricks;

d. Trickle vents;

e. Windows that are not draughty and capable of being opened;

f. Properly installed drainage;

g. External fabric kept in good repair to avoid rain penetration;

h. Properly ventilated roof and under floor spaces to ensure timber remains air dry;

i. Adequate extraction of moisture during peak times, like cooking, bathing and laundry;

j. Efficient heating system appropriate for the thermal properties of the building;

k. Continuous low level ventilation;

l. Using a mechanical heat recovery ventilation ('MHRV') to increase air change rate without the same heat loss. There may be no need for additional background ventilation where windows are ill-fitting, no draught stripping. Where there is draught-stripping, or tight fitting windows, provision for background ventilation may be necessary via trickle vents in replacement windows, insertion of high-level airbricks, or MHRV system.

As set out aforesaid there are many variables, such as design, condition and repair of the dwelling, as well as location and weather, room sizes, how the dwelling is used, patterns of occupants, the number of occupants and possessions etc. What preventative measures may be taken to effectuate change is subject to those variables and causes. Condensation, for example may be less to do with the thermal efficiency of the dwelling and more due to the way in which occupancy use the dwelling and what they do in it.

Excess Heat

This can have the effect of causing cardio-vascular strains and trauma and strokes. Dehydration often arises in tandem with excess heat. There is also the risk of increasing genitourinary diseases.

It concerns temperatures over 25 C.

When considering the likelihood of this hazard, it is important to consider:

a. The age – over 65 year olds are most affected

b. Whether there is provision for natural ventilation, particularly at night or when there are clouds in the sky at night trapping hot air circulating during they day;

c. Air controlling system/s such as air conditioning units or summer bypass units on whole MVHR systems;

d. Type of glazing – solar heat may drive up temperatures;

e. Extent and location of insulation if there is any;

f. Whether ventilation can be controlled or not.

Cause:

a. Poor ventilation;

b. South facing windows;

c. Faulty heating system/s.

Preventative measures include:

a. Natural ventilation;

b. Controllable heating systems;

c. Use of blinds;

d. Open windows;

e. Install blinds or shutters.

Excess Cold

This covers threats to health when temperatures fall below the minimum satisfactory levels for relatively long periods.

A healthy indoor temperature is around 21°C.

Below 16°C, there are serious health risks for the elderly, including respiratory and cardiovascular conditions.

Below 10°C there is a greater risk of hypothermia, especially for the elderly.

Excess cold can also cause an increase in blood pressure and reduce resistance to infection because of the effect of cold air on bronchial lining.

When considering the likelihood of this hazard, it is important to consider

a. Age – over 65-year-olds are the most vulnerable or young children whose thermoregulatory system is immature;

b. The time of year – there are excess winter deaths because of changes in outdoor temperature as well as seasonal infections, air pollution level changes etc;

c. The location of the dwelling (wet, damp part of England);

d. The energy efficiency and what installations are in place to prevent excess cold as well as the type of heating provision and size;

e. The way the dwelling is used;

f. Regard for the dwelling energy rating using SAP (Standard Assessment Procedure for Energy Rating of Dwellings, 2001, BRE, Watford)

Cause:

a. changes in outdoor temperature among other factors;

b. Sleeping in cold bedrooms;

c. Poor insulation;

d. low energy efficiency;

e. inefficient heating systems;

f. excessive damp;

g. less effective insulating material like glass fibre

Preventive measures include:

a. thermal insulation to minimise heat loss subject to location and proximity to other buildings;

b. appropriately installed heating system that is safe, maintained and capable of being controlled by occupant/s;

c. low-level background ventilation without too much heat loss/draughts and which is capable of being controlled by occupant/s;

d. air bricks and windows that can open;

e. means of rapid ventilation;

f. suitable installed floorboards, doors and encasements

Non-Microbial

Asbestos and Manufactured Mineral Fibres ('MMF')

This is concerns the presence of and exposure to asbestos fibres and Manufactured Mineral Fibres ('MMF') such as glass fibre in dwellings.

Asbestos is a natural mineral fibre known more specifically as Chrysotile, amosite and crocidolite. These are fire resistant and used to be used frequently as insulation material.

When considering the likelihood of this hazard, it is important to consider:

a. no age group is more vulnerable than others but smokers are at an increased risk of developing lung cancer when exposed to asbestos;

b. as to asbestos, the health implications tend to occur a long time (approximately 10 years) after first exposure and arise in circumstances where there has been an inhalation of asbestos fibres. Damage can be caused to the lungs such as to the pleura. In some instances, it can cause fibrosis and plaques which, over time (20 to 50 years) can lead to more serious conditions such as cancer;

c. as to MMF, this is an irritant to eyes, skin and respiration system. Occasionally it can cause dermatitis;

d. the date of construction.

Cause:

a. As to asbestos: it is found mostly in traditionally built houses and flats and/or those built as part of the post war building boom and/or high-rise council estates built in the 1950s and 1960s. Fibre levels are low if they are left undisturbed but if work/s are done, then they may become airborne and pose a danger to health subject to the exposure time. Infrequent, short and periodic exposure poses less of a danger than continued exposure over, for example, a week;

b. As to MMF: this is generally found in loft and cavity insulation.

Preventative measures include:

a. Assess whether the asbestos has been disturbed;

b. Where work/s is being carried out, consider the safe removal of asbestos and/or prevention of disruption to the asbestos;

c. Cover or otherwise protect and/or seal the MMF and/or asbestos where practicable to do so in the absence of removing the same;

d. Record where the MMF and asbestos is;

e. In the event that the asbestos is to be removed, it should be done by a contractor licensed by the Health and Safety Executive ('HSE').

__Biocides__

This means insecticides and similar but not inclusive of pest infestations.

No specific age group is affected by the same.

Inhalation is the main risk that arises and, in young children, ingestion.

Cause:

a. Inadequate fumigation

Preventative measures include:

a. Ensuring that what is used is UK approved;

b. Ensuring that the dwelling is ventilated and/or occupants are decanted until the air is cleared.

Carbon Monoxide, Nitrogen dioxide and sulphur dioxide and Fuel Combustion Products

These are associated with the combustion or incomplete combustion of gas and oil.

The 65 year plus age group is most vulnerable.

It is colourless and odourless but extremely toxic. It can cause unconsciousness and death. Headaches, dizziness, nausea and confusion are common.

Nitrogen and Sulphur tend to cause damage to the lining of the lungs and airways. They contribute to bacterial and viral infections.

Cause:

a. Defective appliance/s;

b. Inadequate ventilation;

c. Open flued appliances;

d. Vehicle exhausts (integral garages);

e. Flueless gas or oil heaters.

Preventative measures include:

a. Install carbon monoxide alarms;

b. Regular gas testing of supply and appliances;

c. Adequate ventilation;

d. Install a lobby between a garage and living accommodation.

Lead

Those under three are most at risk.

It is typically found in dwellings on and/or in and/or makes up the paint and water pipes. If the dwelling is on or built near contaminated land, it can also be found in the soil.

If the dwelling is near a busy road exhaust fumes can be the source (though leaded petrol is less common with the rise or hybrid and electric).

Lead, if ingested, affects iron and calcium absorption.

It can affect young children neurologically.

Cause:

a. Paint;

b. Water pipes;

c. Soil near or on contaminated land;

d. Busy roads;

e. Dwellings built pre 1960s that have the original paint.

Preventative measures include:

a. Do not buy lead paint;

b. Strip and replace lead paint.

Radiation

Low frequency current from power lines, sub-stations and appliances.

High frequency current from telephone masts, tv and radio transmitters, microwave ovens and radar.

Leakage from microwave ovens is the most common of these in dwellings.

Two forms of emission mean that it is either ionising or non-ionising. The decay of radon over time can pass through the tissues of the body and damage DNA to cause genetic mutation. Non-ionising radiation does not cause such damage.

Radon is the second most important cause of lung cancer after smoking. Radon is something that is now searched pre purchase of a dwelling.

Causes:

a. Natural sources practically where the underlying rock is granite;

b. Indoor levels depend on how the property is heated and ventilated.

Preventative measures include:

a. Install a radon barrier if it is a natural source and it is high;

b. Regularly ventilate;

c. Regularly test the microwave oven and check its seals;

d. Check any private water supply if from a well or borehole.

Uncombusted fuel gas

Fuel gases can cause asphyxiation. This is where gas builds up in a swelling, it displaces the oxygen levels and if oxygen drops to 14% or less, asphyxiation is likely.

Cause:

a. Mains gas;

b. Dwellings using LPG (liquid petroleum gas).

Preventative measures include:

a. Pressure regulators installed;

b. Regularly service appliances;

c. Adequate low level ventilation if one is using LPG;

d. Install gas detectors.

Organic Compounds

These are chemicals which are gaseous at room temperature.

Irritation and headaches are most common.

Cause:

a. Plywood, chipboard;

b. Paints, solvents and glues;

c. Cleaning products.

Preventative measures include:

a. Ventilate the property when working on or using these materials.

Psychological

<u>*Crowding*</u>

There is no specific age group.

Often socio-economic factors play a part.

Lack of space and overcrowded conditions can result in greater condensation and damp, reduced tolerance, lack of privacy, disruption to sleep and ability to concentrate on homework etc.

During the Covid-19 pandemic this was not uncommon for many.

There should be sufficient space for social interaction while allowing others private time away from other household members.

Privacy is important for young adult going through puberty.

Cause:

a. Too many belongings;

b. Too many people with limited means to move somewhere bigger.

Preventative measures include:

a. Sufficient space for different household activities;

b. Physical separation between the living areas and sleeping areas;

c. As a guide, a dwelling containing two bedrooms is suitable for up to 4 persons;

d. Outdoor play space should be visible to the dwelling;

e. Ensuring there is a door to personal washing areas and which are appropriately sized.

Entry by intruders

There is no specific age group that is more vulnerable than another.

It can cause stress, anxiety, fear and injury to those who are victims of aggravated burglary.

Fear of burglary arises out of one's own experience or hearing of it from someone they know.

Physical attributes of the dwelling are significant:

a. Is there a communal front door to a bock of flats that is sufficiently secure or it constantly broken?

b. Is there security?

c. Is there a concierge?

d. CCTV cameras installed and used;

e. Are locks on the appropriate windows and doors, and do they work?

Cause:

a. Inadequate locking mechanisms on doors and windows (or none at all);

b. Items left on show;

c. Expensive cars parked in drives;

d. Insufficient lighting making it easier to go undetected on break in;

e. Leaving windows open in the summer.

Preventative measures include:

a. Providing separate space for the dwelling to the public areas;

b. The dwelling itself should be capable of being secured against unauthorised entry;

c. Use window locks, burglar alarms, security lighting, chains on doors, fencing;

d. Keep keys out of sight and all expensive items away from view. This includes car keys;

e. Leaving car keys in a box which prevents the signal;

f. Regularly test entry phones

Lighting

Inadequate lighting can cause depression, eye strain and disturbance.

Intrusive lighting includes artificial external lighting.

Cause:

a. Layout and shapes of rooms;

b. Adequacy of curtains and blinds;

c. Size of foliage outside windows;

d. Close proximity to commercial buildings that leave lights on when not in use;

e. Crane lights on building sites;

f. Street lights;

g. Security lighting.

Preventative measures include:

a. More lamps and different lightbulbs;

b. Blackout blinds;

c. Wide enough windows;

d. Low window sills;

e. Pruning large foliage;

f. Lodging complaints with the local authority if the foliage is in contravention of Part 8 of the Anti-social Behaviour Act 2003 and the High Hedges (Appeals) (England) Regulations 2005.

Noise

No specific age group is more vulnerable than others.

Hearing loss and impairment can occur as can lack of concentration and the development of sleep disorders. The increased stress can also cause heightened blood pressure and headaches. If it is at night cortisol levels increase.

Cause:

a. Traffic;

b. Airports;

c. Music from neighbours;

d. Building work;

e. Communal doors or neighbours doors with no door closers;

f. Arguments and shouting.

Preventative measures include:

a. Triple glazing;

b. Greater internal and external insulation;

c. Door closer;

d. Earplugs.

Protection Against Infection

Pests, Domestic Hygiene and refuse

No age group is more vulnerable than another.

Common ailments that arise due to poor hygiene and pests include:

a. Allergic reactions;

b. Asthma;

c. Bronchitis;

d. Gastro-intestinal disease;

e. Depression and anxiety;

f. Bites;

g. Wasted food spoiled by pests;

h. Campylobacter;

i. E-Coli;

j. Salmonella

Cause:

a. Poor design and layout;

b. Access into and within the dwelling for pests;

c. Location of rubbish stores and/or chutes;

d. Proximity to rail lines, canals and rivers;

e. Inadequate provision for storing and disposing of household waste;

f. Cross contamination by pests carrying a disease infecting food and surfaces;

g. Inadequately maintained sewers.

Preventative measures include:

a. Repairing service ducts and holes where pests can get into the dwelling;

b. Treatment of the infestation to ensure there is no reinfection;

c. No cracked walls and surfaces;

d. Regular cleaning;

e. Design and construction should avoid access by pests;

f. Openings into drains should be sealed with an effective water seal;

g. Any holes needed for ventilation should be covered with grilles;

h. Suitable and sufficient storage for food including sufficient surface for preparation of food;

i. Clear and defined area for refuse containers;

j. Fix damaged drains and sewers;

k. Replace ill fitting doors and windows.

Food Safety

There is no specific age group that is more vulnerable than another.

Common ailments that arise include:

a. Gastro-intestinal disease;

b. Depression and anxiety;

c. Wasted food;

d. Campylobacter;

e. E-Coli;

f. Salmonella.

Causes:

a. Food can become a source of food poisoning if left uncovered or left in a fridge that is not adequately cold.

b. Sinks that are used for washing and preparing food is often a source of cross contamination.

Preventative measures include:

a. Providing adequate storage;

b. Installing and maintaining dishwasher, space permitting;

c. Cleaning surfaces regularly;

d. Oven cleaning;

e. Seal joints in and around the sink;

f. Ensure appliances such as fridges and freezers are set to and are maintained at the correct temperature;

g. Smooth drainer with no grooves presents less chance of bugs and virus harbouring cracks;

h. Sufficient number of power sockets;

i. Ensure surfaces of smooth;

j. Ensure there is a drainer to the sink;

k. Suitably sized hob and oven;

l. Sufficient ventilation for smells, condensation.

Personal Hygiene, Sanitation and Drainage

This tends to affect children under 5 years of age.

Skin infections, gastro-intestinal infection and stomach upset is common. This includes rotavirus and dysentery.

Causes:

a. Sharing facilities;

b. Damaged macerator and waste pipes;

c. Leaking cisterns;

d. Inadequate flushing mechanism;

e. Obsolete water closets.

Preventative measures include:

a. Working flushing cistern;

b. Water basin should ensure there is a supply of water and is properly connected to the drain capable of safely carrying the waste out of the dwelling;

c. Toilet basins should be securely fixed and be capable of carrying a person's weight;

d. The flushing cistern lever or button must be made of material cleansable material;

e. Safe supply of electricity if a macerator is installed;

f. Adequately ventilate the bathroom/sanitary accommodation;

g. There should be a sufficient number of baths or showers for the number of potential occupants. They must be strong enough to take a person's weight;

h. Ensure adequately sized waste pipes are installed;

i. All connections must be sealed and air-tight to avoid leakage;

j. Ensure there is sufficient clothes drying facilities.

Water Supply

This concerns the quality and adequacy of the supply of water.

Microbiological pathogens that affect drinking water typically cause gastro-intestinal illness.

Legionella causes respiratory infection and is a risk associated with domestic water systems.

Cause:

a. This tends to arise more often where there are private water supplies. Private water supplies are usually pumped into a storage tank within the dwelling;

b. Inadequate filters;

c. Flooding causing the mains water supply to become contaminated when pipes crack.

Preventative measures include:

a. Cover water tanks;

b. Monitor temperature levels in water tanks, especially in the summer;

c. Regular sampling of drinking water to be carried out by water utility providers;

d. Hot water must be maintained above 55 degrees Celsius to prevent legionella;

e. Cold water must be maintained to less than 20 degrees Celsius to prevent legionella;

f. Ensure there is adequate water pressure from the mains water to supply all dwellings;

g. Drinking water for large buildings should be sampled and analysed regularly.

Protection Against Accidents

Falls – baths, fixtures

Those over the age of 60 more vulnerable than others.

Baths, showers, shower trays or similar are associated with the following injuries when one falls on, in or over the same:

a. Cuts;

b. Bruising;

c. Broken or dislocated bones – hips, shoulders, legs;

d. Pneumonia, heart attack or cardio-respiratory illness as a result of being without help and assistance for some time immediately after the fall.

Cause:

a. Lack of grab handles;

b. Lack of bath/shower mats inside and outside the bath, shower or similar facility;

c. Hard floor that one falls onto.

Preventative measures include:

a. Anti-slip mats;

b. Insulated lino floors;

c. Ensure the door to the shower is positioned correctly;

d. Installing such fixtures and sanitary ware in such a way that there is sufficient space to use the same and get in and/or out of it safely – adequate functional space;

e. Sufficient lighting so one can see what they are doing;

f. Install grab handles;

g. Adequate heating;

h. Ensure the fixture, appliance or sanitaryware is fitted securely.

Falling on Level Surfaces

This concerns falls on or over thresholds, steps, paths, yards, driveways, floors.

Those age 60 years or over tend to be most vulnerable compared to others.

Falls can result in injury:

a. Cuts;

b. Bruising;

c. Broken or dislocated bones – hips, shoulders, legs;

d. Pneumonia, heart attack or cardio-respiratory illness as a result of being without help and assistance for some time immediately after the fall;

e. Spinal injury;

f. Sprains;

g. Fractures.

Causes:

a. Uneven surface lacking in slip resistance;

b. Weather dependent – lack of grit in icy weather, rain causing the surface to be slippy underfoot;

c. Floors with a depth of 5mm to 20mm tend to increase the likelihood of a trip;

d. Damp, mould, water ingress causing tiles, wood, or stone floors to crack;

e. Insufficient drainage;

f. Lack of sufficient space to manoeuvre;

g. Thread bare carpets;

h. Lack of lighting.

Preventative measures include:

a. Effective surface water drainage;

b. Reactionary steps during poor weather by using grit or ensuring there is grit readily accessible in the winter months;

c. Regularly maintaining external paths to ensure slip hazards such as moss is not present;

d. Install security lights;

e. Glare from windows should be avoided;

f. Each room should be free from obstructions;

g. Replace carpets and their treads;

h. Remove any sharp edges.

Falling on Stairs

Those over 60 years of age tend to be more vulnerable.

Falls can result in injury:

a. Cuts;

b. Bruising;

c. Broken or dislocated bones – hips, shoulders, legs;

d. Pneumonia, heart attack or cardio-respiratory illness as a result of being without help and assistance for some time immediately after the fall;

e. Spinal injury;

f. Sprains;

g. Fractures.

Stairs include internal stairs, external steps or ramps within the curtilage of the dwelling.

Stairs also include internal communal stairs and ramps as well as external steps or ramps within the curtilage of the building containing the dwelling and giving access to the dwelling.

Cause:

a. Lack of winders or bannisters;

b. Insufficient lighting;

i. Weather dependent – lack of grit in icy weather, rain causing the surface to be slippy underfoot;

c. Pitch of stairs is greater than 42 degrees;

d. Nosings projecting more than 18mm.

Preventative measures include:

a. Tread and rise dimensions of 280-360mm and 100-180mm;

b. Stair width should be at least 900mm so that they can negotiated by a child and adult side by side;

c. Handrails at 900mm and 1000mm from the top of the handrail to the pitch line or floor;

d. Good lighting;

e. There should be reasonable space at the top and bottom of stairs so that one can negotiate them and plan their movements more easily;

f. Ensure the stairs are free from obstructions;

g. Remove sharp edges on stairs and balustrades;

h. Ensure that spindles are not too wide apart that a limb or child can become stuck or fall through.

Falls between levels

Those under the age of 5 tend to be most vulnerable.

This includes falls from balconies, landings, accessible roof, wells and over garden retaining walls.

Injuries include:

a. Cuts;

b. Bruising;

c. Broken or dislocated bones – hips, shoulders, legs;

d. Pneumonia, heart attack or cardio-respiratory illness as a result of being without help and assistance for some time immediately after the fall;

e. Spinal injury;

f. Sprains;

g. Fractures;

h. Death.

Cause:

a. Lack of window restrictors;

b. Leaving windows wide open;

c. Low window sill;

d. The way a window is designed for opening;

e. Aggravating features include what lies below a balcony or window such as fences, bins, cars, busy road, hedge/s, tree/s.

Preventative measures include:

a. Greater lighting;

b. Window restrictors;

c. If a window needs to be kept open for ventilation, have a small window that is capable of being opened from the top with the substantive part of the same remaining closed. 600mm above the floor is likely to be sufficient;

d. Internal sills ought to be at least 1,100mm from the finished floor;

e. Install safety rails;

f. Safe cleaning of the outer surface so that one does not have reason to climb on a chair or stepladder to clean it;

g. Guarding should be provided to balconies and landings.

Electric Shocks, Fires, Burns and Scalds

Those under the age of 5 are most vulnerable.

Burns can occur at the point of contact with the source of electricity. Mild tingling through to contractions of the heart are the most likely injuries.

Cause:

a. Touching metal or other conducting material which is live;

b. Deficient electrical wiring;

c. Overloading circuits;

d. Use of extension leads plugged into each other.

Preventative measures include:

a. Regular PAT testing of appliances;

b. Update wiring consistent with current wiring regulations;

c. Ensure all electrical work is completed by a qualified electrician well versed and qualified in the lates edition of IET wiring regulations;

d. Not installing plugs and sockets near water eg: no sockets in the bathroom other than a 12 volt AC shaver socket;

e. If lightning is a possibility, ensure there is a lightening protection system;

f. If equipment greater than 230 volts is used, ensure it has an RCD.

Fire

Cause:

a. This can be caused by clothes and furniture setting alight;

b. Overloading circuits;

c. Faulty appliances;

d. Smoking and falling asleep or not ensuring the cigarette or cigar has been put out;

e. Covering space heaters with clothes or towels;

f. Chip pan fires;

g. Leaving cooking unattended.

Preventative measures include:

a. Fire alarms;

b. Checking cladding is fire retardant;

c. PAT testing appliances;

d. Updating wiring;

e. Ensure there is adequate heating without the need for portable or space heaters to be used;

f. Install RCDs to help prevent fires associated with electrical deficiencies;

g. Readily available fire blanket and extinguisher;

h. Fire retardant furniture;

i. Self-closer doors;

j. Fire rated doors;

k. Ensure there is sufficient clothes drying facilities so one is not tempted to use a space heater or oil radiator to dry clothes;

l. Not leaving hair dryers or straighteners on if not in use and in any event not leaving them on carpets, beds, clothes or towels;

m. Ensure that integrated dryers are sufficiently ventilated and lint regularly removed.

Flames, hot surfaces

This concerns burns and scalds from hot liquids and vapour.

Those under the age of 5 tend to be the most vulnerable.

Cause:

a. Most accidents happen in the kitchen including hot drinks deep fryers and kettles;

b. Fires and heaters which are touched by children under 5;

c. Cooking in the bedroom or in a cramped space.

Preventative measures include:

a. Guarding open flames such as open fires;

b. Boilers, tanks and hot water tanks limited to a maximum of 43 degrees Celsius;

c. Ensure the kitchen is of adequate size and layout;

d. Install safety gates for young children;

e. If more than household is sharing a kitchen there should be a separate worktop space and separate cooking facilities for each household;

f. Thermostatic taps.

Collisions, Cuts and strains

Collision and Entrapment

This includes cases where body parts are trapped in architectural features such as doors and windows and/or where one collides with a window and it smashes.

Those under the age of 5 are the most vulnerable.

Most accidents tend to involve fingers trapped in doors or smashing of windows by toys or body parts.

Cause:

a. Windows or doors which are difficult to close which require more force;

b. Blind corners in the dwelling;

c. Broken or weak sash cords;

d. Gaps to landings, stairs and balconies which children stick their limbs or head through and become trapped;

e. Areas where there is low headroom.

Preventative measures include:

a. Maintain doors and windows;

b. Safety glazing in vulnerable locations;

c. Maintained sash cords;

d. Ensure self-closers are not too vigorous.

Explosions

This tends to arise when there is a partial or total collapse of a building during building or demolition works.

Injuries include crushing, bruising, broken bones, fractures, and lacerations.

Cause:

a. Stored gas;

b. Demolition near dwellings;

c. Water vapour explosions;

d. Mains gas.

Preventative measures include:

a. Regular testing of gas appliances including central heating;

b. Not installing hot water storage tanks of more than 15 litres to the mains water supply.

Position of Amenities

This concerns the lack of functional space.

Injuries include strains, sprains and broken bones.

Cause:

a. Inadequate space around the bathroom or kitchen facilities;

b. Low headroom;

c. Awkward positioning of windows.

Preventative measures include:

a. Install appliances with sufficient user space;

b. Light switches should be conveniently located;

c. Window latches should be at a reasonable height

Structural Collapse and Falling Elements

This concerns the fabric of the building falling due to inadequate fixing, adverse weather or disrepair.

Cause:

a. Falling slates, bricks, windows, gutters;

b. Collapsed walls;

c. Light fittings not adequately fixed;

d. Cupboard doors not adequately fixed.

Preventative measures include:

a. Ensure load bearing walls can withstand the floor or ceiling it is holding up;

b. Lintels should be of sufficient strength;

c. Coping should be securely fixed;

d. Roof coverings should be securely fixed and can cope with wind and rain;

e. Securely fit gutters and pipes;

f. Regularly clear gutters so they do not collapse from the weight of debris, snow and/or rain.

CHAPTER FIVE

HMOs

There are no exceptions for HMOs

A local authority has a specific duty to consider whether there are category 1 hazards in HMOs which are subject to mandatory licensing. Assessments in relation to such dwellings ought to be carried out as soon as practicable after a licence application has been received and no later than five years.

The HHSRS is applied to any form of dwelling whether it is self-contained or not, in

a large building or not. The EHO ought to examine the dwelling inclusive of all its parts and areas, shared or not, which form part of that dwelling.

If rooms are shared, the assessment ought to look at the likelihood and/or outcomes which could happen as a result of the sharing. Factors to consider include:

a. the number of other dwellings sharing rooms and areas;

b. the chance of a risk of infection potentially being greater because of sharing, or

c. whether any of the occupiers is under stress because of the sharing;

d. the type of hazard/s being assessed.

Hazards may be viewed with more care and attention when dealing with HMOs because the type of hazard and its impact may be greater. When judging likelihood and outcomes, the assessor should take into account the increased likelihood of rooms and areas that are shared presenting with a hazard.

The "landlord's" responsibility in rooms and areas which are shared extends further than it does in those areas which are in exclusive occupation. In these rooms and areas, the landlord is also responsible for the furnishing and appliances. This includes floor coverings, cookers, refrigerators, light bulbs etc.

The assessor should also consider passages, corridors, access, landings, balconies. Stairs lifts, any shared rooms and facilities including refuse storage and refuse chutes. Matters relating to management do not fall within the HHRS

Damp

When the hazard considered is damp, subject to the type of enforcement notice served, the occupiers may be confined to one or two more areas until such time when this hazard is resolved and/or are unable to control temperatures within the dwelling without centrally controlled space heating systems. This makes them more vulnerable.

Security

Concierge and caretaker systems may reduce crime.

When assessing the security of the building this calls for an assessment of the whole building security in addition to assessment of security between individual residents in the same building.

Excess heat/cold

HMOs dwellings are more prone to hazards such as:

a. bad insulation;

b. un-insulated roof;

c. heating systems not under the control of the occupier/s.

Insect Pests, hygiene, sanitation, food safety and water supply

HMOs are more vulnerable to certain insect pests, particularly if, when assessed, it becomes apparent that there is no clearly defined area for refuse containers. Such containers ought to be sheltered and away from the elements but still in open air. It should follow that such stores reduce invasion by pests.

In more modern blocks of flats ventilated rubbish chutes are more commonly found. Chutes may be installed for individual flats, but communal chutes are recommended for HMOs of more than four-storeys.

Equally important is considering whether there is a higher risk of infection where there is a higher number of people sharing facilities which in turn can pose a danger to food safety and/or lack of safe food practice and/or communication in respect of the same, as well as the increased risk of infection when sharing personal hygiene/sanitation facilities. This includes regard for the ratio of facilities to occupants.

When considering water supply, it is important for the EHO to assess the temperature of water in pipes, cisterns, taps and vessels.

Fire safety

When considering whether a dwelling is at threat from accidental fire, regard must be had to the type of dwelling and its age. Factors or awareness of the same include:

a. fires are more common in flats;

b. dwelling constructed post 1980 have a lower likelihood of fire;

c. whether there is emergency lighting, sprinkles, adequate means of escape and interconnected fire detection and/or alarm system;

d. whether there is fire separation between each dwelling.

Such considerations are particularly important since the Grenfell Tower tragedy.

Section 55 of the Housing Act 2004

The HMO licensing regime provides local authorities with procedures to assess the fitness of a person to be a licence-holder and consider the suitability of the property for the number of occupants proposed.

A HHSRS assessment does not form a part of the licensing procedure but pursuant to section 55, authorities must be satisfied that not later than 5 years after an application for a licence has been received that there are no Part 1 functions that ought to be exercised in relation to premises in respect of which the licensing application is made.

The licensing process may cause the authority to prioritise certain properties in order to mitigate possible hazards.

However, where all matters in relation to the application for a licence as per section 64(3)

of the Housing Act2004 are satisfied, the authority should not unreasonably delay the grant of a licence pending its consideration of its duties or powers under Part 1.

Licensing decisions in relation to the maximum number of occupants who may occupy the HMO will not always be influenced by a prohibition under Part 1. However, where the authority considers that the condition of an HMO is such that it might take action under Part 1 to prohibit the use of an HMO or restrict occupancy, it may proceed with the licence subsequently.

CHAPTER SIX

CLADDING

This chapter looks at how the HHSRS operates post-Grenfell

ACM

Since Grenfell Tower in 2017, it has been found[2] that Aluminium Composition Materials ('ACM') cladding systems represent a fire hazard.

Type of Hazard

The presence of ACM or any other cladding or filler that is combustible is considered as deficiencies contributing to the hazard (fire).

The advice on fire safety is from the Ministry for Housing, Communities, and Local

Government (MHCLG) independent expert advisory panel[3] is that:

a. any wall system containing an ACM category 3 cladding panel, even when combined with limited combustibility insulation material, does not meet current Building Regulations guidance,

[2] The government appointed an independent expert panel to provide advice to the Secretary of State for Communities and Local Government, on immediate building safety measures following the Grenfell Tower fire. The expert panel's advice can be found at: https:// www.gov.uk/government/collections/building-safety-independent-expert-advisory-panel

[3] https://www.gov.uk/government/collections/building-safety-independent-expert-advisory-panel

and it is not aware of any tests of such combinations meeting the standard set by BR1357

b. Wall systems with these materials therefore present a significant fire hazard on buildings over 18m.

A local housing authority undertaking an inspection of a high-rise building will need to ascertain whether the wall system is correctly installed and maintained, as well as meeting BS8414-1 and 2.

Inspection

Common parts will need to be inspected to determine if there is a risk of cladding. Technically the Housing Act 2004 permits inspection and rating of common parts as separate to residential premises, but it is now understood that the common parts of a high-rise will include the exterior (as well as cladding), and internal common parts of each floor such as the stairways and hallways. Regards may also be had to terraces, communal gardens and private balconies. The latter maybe part of an individual dwelling but by its very nature it also forms part of the exterior common parts and is therefore relevant to the question if any spread of fire.

This does not mean that all dwellings need to be inspected when assessing the common parts.

The difficulty is knowing whether a deficiency exists when looking at cladding. An HHSRS inspection in relation to fire will not confirm whether some deficiencies exist (for example the form, structure and fixing of cladding and fire cavity barriers). Any rating is likely to be provisional pending either detailed testing or a copy of relevant information, such as an up-to-date testing report.

For the avoidance of doubt, the existence of waking watches is irrelevant.

Fire and Rescue Authorities

Section 10 of the Housing Act 2004 requires local housing authorities to consult the local fire and rescue authority before taking enforcement action in respect of a prescribed fire hazard in an HMO or in the common parts of a building containing flats.

Where the authority intends to take emergency measures, the duty to consult applies only so far as it is practicable to do so before taking the action.

There is a difference between "common parts" in the Housing Act 2004 and definitions used in the Regulatory Reform (Fire Safety) Order 2005 (which instead describes areas "used in common by the occupants of more than one such dwelling).

In order to comply with the duties imposed by the Fire Safety Order, the responsible person must carry out a fire risk assessment to identify what fire hazards exist at the premises and what measures have been taken (or will be taken) to minimise the risk in the parts of buildings containing flats and maisonettes that are used in common.

Profile

The HHSRS Hazard profile for fire notes that smoke and gas can pass through a building with insufficient damping in ventilation systems, flaming droplets and delamination of cladding.

Uncontrolled fire can have a number of health effects, both direct and indirect. Direct outcomes include burn injuries which, when severe, can be life-changing or life-threatening and the most extreme (Class 1 harms). Asphyxiation from gas or smoke is also a health effect to consider.

Cause

Cladding itself may not be a cause but it may hasten the spread. The MHCLG Expert Panel's advice following large scale testing is that ACM with an unmodified polyethylene filler or core (category 3 in screening tests) with any type of insulation presents a significant hazard on buildings over 18m[4].

Causes and exacerbating factors to consider as well as the subsequent harm when assessing a fire hazard with the potential presence of cladding or otherwise are numerous and include:

a. Ignition of fire – bbqs on balconies, burning wood, smoking;

b. Design, material and construction of a building failing to limit the spread of fire;

c. Insufficient or blocked fire escapes and inadequate safety plans;

d. The stay put principle is not designed to be put in place in buildings with insufficient compartmentation such as fire safety doors with minimum time limits;

e. Smoke control system not functioning such as not activating sprinklers if there are any, activation of sealed windows to be opened and sounding an alarm that can be heard throughout the entire building;

f. Lack of current suitable Fire Risk Assessment;

g. Inadequate or absent record of dry riser (or wet riser);

h. Degree of compartmentation;

---

[4]https://assets.publishing.service.gov.uk/government/uploads/system/uploads/attachment_data/file/684350/20180228_-_Update_and_consolidated_advice_for_building_owners_following_large-scale_testing.pdf

i. What is in fire resistant enclosures and what is not such as rubbish holds;

j. Where the sources of fuel are that are flammable;

k. Lack of security to prevent arson;

l. Obstructions such as prams and door mats;

m. Absence of emergency lighting;

n. Absence of or limited access for firefighters separate to the escape for occupants;

o. Extent of signage explaining what to do;

p. Distance between building and evacuation point;

q. Existence of evacuation chairs, or lack of.

The MHCLG Expert Panel's advice following large scale testing is that ACM with an unmodified polyethylene filler or core (category 3 in screening tests) with any type of insulation presents a significant hazard on buildings over 18m[14]. The issue of partial cladding, such as decorative panels has also been addressed in MHCLG advice to building owners[15] which said that "the clearest way to ensure the safety of residents is to remove all ACM, including small or partial areas of ACM, and replace it with a safe material. This remains the most appropriate remediation solution".

When considering the likelihood, factors include:

a. Presence of combustible cladding increasing the likelihood of fire spreading but itself will not affect the likelihood of a fire starting;

b. Whether there is combustible cladding or not, regard must be had to other factors named above;

c. What the means of escape are.

The harm caused is not isolated to physical harm or loss of life. It is now recognised that there are mental health impacts too. The latter us unlikely to be a Class 1 harm outcome over the first 12 months but it will increase to Class II and III Outcomes.

CHAPTER SEVEN

FORMAL ENFORCEMENT OPTIONS

This chapter looks at the various options for formal enforcement

Part 3 of the Environmental Protection Act 1990 ('EPA 1990') gives local authorities powers to require the abatement of several issues, including where the physical state of premises amounts to a statutory nuisance (section 79).

Much of this legislation can be used by tenants, occupiers and/or their neighbours to force work/s to be done to improve the condition of the property. Part 3 is concerned with tackling the effects of bad housing. This is particularly useful if the property is unhealthy or otherwise in poor condition but there is no civil remedy because there is no breach of contract or any other civil 'wrong.' There is no restriction on who can raise a complaint about conditions with the local authority and request an inspection under the Housing Act 2004 (section 3(3)(a), ('HA 2004').

Procedure

If the local authority considers that it would be appropriate to inspect the property under Part 1 of the HA 2004, then it must arrange for an inspection to be carried out pursuant to section 4(2). The local authority should ensure that their contact details are publicly available and accessible.

The local authority should act within a reasonable period of time because a failure to do so may lead to an 'official complaint' to be lodged by a justice of the peace for the area pursuant to section 4. This is not the same as the local housing authority's complaint procedure. Should the local authority receive an official complaint it is bound to consider the report from the inspecting officer if the inspecting officer is of the view that a hazard exists (section 4(6)) and inspect the property pursuant to section 4(2). Whilst there is no statutory timetable within which the local authority must respond to official complaints it should attend to the same and inspect the property as soon as possible (section 4(6) (7)). Thereafter, any delay will leave judicial review open to the applicant where a mandatory order may be obtained to require the local authority to act.

It is sometimes the case that the local authority has tried to access the property but has been prevented from doing so. One of the most important elements of an inspection for HHSRS purposes is section 239(5) Housing Act 2004. The local authority may, in that event, consider applying for an injunction or exercise its powers of entry pursuant to section 239(3) of the HA 2004.

Section 239

Notice of at least 24 hours should be given if powers of entry are to be exercised but if there is reasonable concern that there is a certain offence being committed or that emergency remedial action is required, then immediate access may be obtained under section 239(3) without giving prior notice, see subsections 5 and 6. Any hesitation to not use legal powers available to it would be frowned upon in the Administrative Division of the High Court in the event that an application for judicial review is made.

Section 239(9) sets out that the purpose of attendance be set out in any notice served.

Information should also include the postal address, email and telephone number for the department and who the owner/occupier should contact about the notice and/or other communications relevant to it. Without this correspondence information clearly set out in or appended to the notice, an owner and/or occupier is deprived of the information necessary to contact the correct department. It defeats the object of having such notices if such information is not provided.

As is stated in *Williams v Monmouthshire County Council (RPT/HA04/S11 Imp/8)* paragraph 5:

> *"It seems clear that Parliament intended that the owner and occupier should be given notice so that they could attend and make representations if necessary because of the potential gravity of the enforcement powers".*

In *Evans v London Borough of Camden (LON/00AG/HIN/2007/0009)* at paragraph 13 it was stated:

> *"The Tribunal is also of the opinion that the purpose of Section 239(5) is to give a mandatory warning to occupiers and owners of an inspection and some opportunity to deal with it before inspection and the service of a notice".*

Therefore, if, for example, the date and time of inspection is not convenient for the owner and/or occupier, the owner and/or occupier does not know who to contact and it would be incorrect to assume that all owners and/or occupiers will have the knowledge to know which department sent the notice and the means to research for themselves the phone number, email and/or postal address.

Further or alternatively, the time spent researching the correct department to contact and their details is not necessarily time that the owner and/or occupier may have available to them if the time period given is only 24 hours (and the notice is served on the morning before). If an owner and/or occupier is working a full-time day, for example, and does not read their post until after they return and after the Council department has closed for the day, the only immediate method of communication available to them is email. One would hope that this would be read before the relevant officers attend the property. Therefore, knowing what the email address is might be convenient for the owner and/or occupier to use to notify the relevant department if the next morning is not possible.

Moreover, it would be incorrect to assume that even with time to research or contact the main switchboard, the owner and/or occupier will get through to the relevant department and the message of the date being inconvenient is relayed. If, however, the relevant correspondence address, email and phone number is given there can be less doubt as to whether the message has indeed been relayed to the relevant officers.

In the absence of a postal address or email address being included on or with the notice, the owner and/or occupier is deprived of his or her opportunity to send correspondence in writing to the correct department. The owner and/or occupier might prefer to have all communication recorded in writing or they might be hard of hearing and feel unable to use a telephone to communicate. This might also be why calling the main switchboard may not be an option to an owner and/or occupier.

Section 239(8)(a) does allow for the assessor to bring any person with him or her but the wording of section 239, when taken with section 243, means that each officer has to be individually authorised to enter to investigate a complaint and identify hazards under section 4

Section 243 requires that the authorisation is given by a deputy chief officer within the meaning of section 2 of the Local Government and Housing Act 1989.

For the avoidance of doubt, section 101 of the Local Government Act 1972 is not referred to therein.

Section 101 cannot be read into section 243 because section 101 is '*subject to any express provision*' contained in any Act passed after the Local Government Act 1972. In other words, if there is an express provision setting out how and who in a local authority discharges any of the local authority's functions, section 101 cannot be invoked, relied on, implied or inferred.

Section 243 of the Housing Act 2004 is an express provision. It is expressly clear that authorisation is given by a Deputy Chief Officer within the meaning of section 2 of the Local Government and Housing Act 1989.

Therefore, it would contradict the preliminary sentence of section 101(1) if, despite being expressly clear that authorisation lies only with the Deputy Chief Officer, section 101 is read into section 243. Being as expressly clear as it is, section 243 removes any scope for local authorities to delegate functions to committees, sub-committees or officers.

In addition, a Deputy Chief Officer is defined at section 2(8) of the Local Government and Housing Act 1989 as:

> *"(8) .... subject to the following provisions of this section, a person who, as respects all or most of the duties of his post, is required to report directly or is directly accountable to one or more of the statutory or non-statutory chief officers."*

Pursuant to section 239(9) an authorisation for the purposes of section 239:

> *"(a) must be in writing; and*
>
> *(b) must state the particular purpose or purposes for which the entry is authorised."*

Courses of Action

There are different enforcement actions available on completion of an assessment by the EHO:

a. Declaring a clearance area;

b. Issuing an improvement notice;

c. Making a prohibition order;

d. Making a demolition order;

e. Hazard awareness notice.

Only one course of action can be taken at any one time.

Declaring a clearance area

This is where the residential buildings in an area contains a category 1 hazard and non-residential buildings in the same area are dangerous. This was principally aimed at slums but can also be used to address areas of unsatisfactory housing. One may be compensated or rehoused by the local authority if this happens.

A clearance area is an area to be cleared of all buildings. (section 289 of the Housing Act 1985 as amended by section 47 of the HA 2004):

a. Each residential building has a category 1 hazard; or

b. Residential buildings in the area are too dangerous or are harmful to health and safety of inhabitants in the areas or;

c. Each residential building contains a category 2 hazard but is in an areas that is dangerous or harmful to the health and safety of inhabitants in the areas and the secretary of state has considered the circumstances of the case in an order;

This normally results in compulsory purchase acquisitions and the clearing of the site in readiness for renewal.

Improvement notice

This requires the recipient of the notice to address the hazards identified, and for such work/s to not start earlier than 28 days after service of the notice (*Odeniran v Southend-on-Sea BC [2013] EWHC 3888 (Admin), [2014] HLR 11*. Statutorily prescribed information must be

included pursuant to section 13.

Prohibition order

This prohibits the use of the property for such categorises of use as the order describes pursuant to section 20. It must set out the hazard and action need before the order can be revoked.

Demolition order

The procedures for this is set out in Part 9 of the Housing Act 1985 and 'demolition order' is defined therein at section 265, as amended by section 46 of the HA 2004.

This order requires the owner to demolish the property after it has been vacated and the site cleared. This means that the property ceases to be used for human habitation.

Hazard awareness notice

This is a notification to the recipient of the existence of Category 1 and/or 2 hazard/s. It is a formal notice to forewarn a recipient that they might consider it wise to remedy the same.

Emergency Action/s

This arises where there is an 'imminent risk of serious harm' this can include entering the property to carry out emergency works pursuant to sections 40 to 42 of the HA 2004. Service of a notice of emergency remedial action is given pursuant to section 40 of the HA 2004.

Environmental Protection Act 1990 ('EPA 1990')

The provisions of Part 3 in the EPA 1990 are wide enough to cover issues such as pest infestation. A problem with fleas is deemed to be the responsibility of the tenant or leaseholder. Therefore, if a local authority's pest control service undertakes to resolve a flea infestation, the authority can recover incurred costs from the occupier, although the service can use its discretion as to whether to charge.

The EPA 1990 also gives local authorities a power of entry to determine if a statutory nuisance exists or to undertake works to prevent such a nuisance (schedule 3). In the context of a domestic property, notice should generally be given before entry is attempted.

Statutory nuisances include:

a. Any premiss in such a state as to be prejudicial to health or a nuisance (section 79(1)(a));

b. Any accumulation or deposit which is prejudicial to health or a nuisance (section 79(1)(e)).

<u>Section 79(1)(a)</u>

Premises is defined to include all land and vessels, occupied or not. Private rented and social housing are covered. In *Birmingham CC v Oakley [2000] UKHL 59; [2001] 33 HLR 283*, the courts have held that EPA 1990 is concerned with the condition of the property, not the way it is used. This means that any enforcement taken under this Act will not necessarily prevent the problem arising again if the root cause is not addressed. It is a sticking plaster and management of consequences only.

Premises includes individuals flats as well as entire blocks of flats. It includes an open site without permanent buildings such as travellers' sites. The statutory nuisance arises if the premises as a whole is in such as state as to be prejudicial to health or is a nuisance. The aim, therefore, is restricted to public health matters.

To be prejudicial to health the statutory nuisance arises where the property (premises) is in such a state, whether due to disrepair, a latent defect or otherwise, as to be prejudicial to health. This means to be 'injurious to likely to cause injury, to health' (section 79(7)) This is an objective test and includes potential, as well as actual ill health. This includes those who are already ill but their condition is likely to deteriorate further as a result of the state and condition of the property, see *Malton Bourgh Health Board v Malton Farmers Manure Co (1879) 4*

Ex D 302. It not confined to physical health but includes mental health as well.

To be a nuisance it must be a public nuisance or private nuisance at common law, see *National Coal Board v Neath BC [1976] 2 All ER 478, DC* that explains the distinction:

a. Public: act or omission that adversely affects the comfort and quality of the public or class of people;

b. Private: substantial interference with the use and enjoyment of neighbouring property. The damage suffered need not be continuing, see *Wandsworth London Borough Council v Railtrack plc [2002] QB 756, [2002] 2 WLR 512, CA.*

Most importantly, the nuisance must relate to matters of public health, *Coventry CC v Cartwright [1975] 1 WLR 845; [1975] 2 All ER 99, DC.* The failure to act does not mean that the defendant must carry out extensive investigations to discover the harm or potential harm. The duty is owed only if there is foreseeability and proximity of harm, as well as whether the duty itself is fair, just and reasonable considering the individual concerned such as whether they are labouring under a disability or disorder.

Schedule 3, paragraph 2 of the EPA 1990 permits an EHO to enter and inspect a property which may in such a state as to be a statutory nuisance. Steps to be taken must be those that are regarded as reasonably practicable.

A local authority may find that one may approach it to request what is called environmental information pursuant to the Environmental Information Regulation 2004 (SI No 3391) regulation 2. There are two exceptions at regulation 12:

a. Standalone exceptions;

b. Adverse effect exceptions.

Nevertheless, the statutory presumption is in favour of disclosure pursuant to regulation 12(2).

Enforcement

Informal Notice

If the EHO is satisfied that there is a statutory nuisance (or it likely to arise), then the local authority is bound to take action, see *Cocker v Cardwell (1869) LR 5 QB 15.*

Practitioners may choose to serve an informal notice first and it is noticeable that some local authorities have their own enforcement protocols. If an informal notice is sent it is suggested that there notice set out what the consequences could be if the nuisance is not abated and/or removed and/or the cause is not resolved With a hoarder, however this is unlikely to be acted upon because they do not necessarily see that they have a problem giving rise toa statutory nuisance in the first place.

A more formal approach would be to serve a abatement notice pursuant to section 80(1) of the EPA 1990. This requires the abatement of the nuisance and any works necessary for that purpose within a specified timeframe. For the avoidance of doubt, this is not a preliminary step to court proceedings. The notice must be clear and enable the recipient to understand what is required. The penal sanctions must also be clearly set out in the event if non-compliance. If certain work/s are suggested then these must be capable of being remedied, see *Network Housing Association Ltd v Westminster CC [1994] Times, 14 April, CA*, even though the local authority has a choice about what notice to serve if any, see *Budd v Colchester Borough Council [1999] Env LR 739, CA.*

Abatement Notice

The abatement notice must be served on the person responsible for the nuisance (section 80(2)(a), as inserted by section 86 of the Clean Neighbourhoods and Environment Act 2005). Pursuant to section 79(7) this is the person to whose act, default or suffer the nuisance is attributable

If the hazards/s is causing or is itself structural damage, the notice must be served on the owner (section 80(2)(b)). If the property is being used to hoard items and the hoarder cannot themselves be located, and the person upon whom to serve the notice, then the local authority must serve the notice on the occupier or owner (depending on the nature of the hoarder's occupation (tenant or owner)), section 80(2)(c),

If there is more than one person responsible, which may be the case of a couple that are hoarders, then the notice may be served on each person whether or not their conduct or default alone would amount to a nuisance, section 81(1).

Once served with such a notice, one has the right to appeal to the magistrates' court within 21 days of the date of service of the notice., section 80(3). This is by way of a complaint. Pursuant to schedule 3 paragraph 1(2).

The basis on which one may appeal is set out in the Statutory Nuisance (Appeals) Regulations 1995 SI No 2644 as amended by SI No 771 (2006). Examples include:

a. Equality Act 2010 – failure to consider that the individual served is labouring under a mental disability that is causing them to hoard;

b. Not served on the correct party;

c. Errors in the notice;

d. Mental Capacity Act 2005 – the individual/s served lacks the capacity to understand what has been served and/or but for their lacking of capacity, would not hoard and cause the subsequent nuisance (private or public).

If the notice is not appeal or is not complied with, then the person served is guilty of an offence unless there is a reasonable excuse. The local authority does not have to prosecute for a failure to comply with such a notice, but the option is there.

If the offence of a failure to comply is proven, then the person liable to a fine up to level 5 on the standard scale and a further fine of one-tenth the level 5 scale for each day after conviction of non-compliance, section 80(5). For the avoidance of doubt, level 5 is an unlimited fine, as amended by section 85 of the Legal Aid, Sentencing and Punishment of Offenders Act ('LASPO') 2012.

An authority can also apply for a High Court injunction where an abatement notice would by itself be inadequate (section 81).

Where an abatement notice is not complied with, a local authority can abate the nuisance itself by carrying out the necessary works and recharging reasonable expenses to the person responsible (section 81(4)). The local authority may choose to serve a notice stating its intention to the do the remedial work/s should the recipient of the abatement notice fail to do so. A period of nine days must be given before the local authority can step in and start doing the works. A counter-notice may be served within 7 days of receipt by recipient of the notice from the local authority. The local authority cannot then do the act/s unless the owner/occupier fails to start remedial work/s within a reasonable period of time or, having started the remedial works, progress has been slow.

Improvement Notice

An improvement notice may be served where a Category 1 or Category 2 hazard exists: section 11 or section 12. The person on whom it is to be served is the same as for a hazard awareness notice. Pursuant to section 13, it must contain the following information:

a. whether the notice is served under section 11 or section 12;

b. the date when the action is to be started and completed by and/or in what tranches;

c. the nature of the hazard and the premises on which it exists, as well as identifying the cause or deficiency;

d. the notice must also contain information about the right to appeal.

An improvement notice requires the person on whom it is served to carry out specified remedial action. In relation to Category 1 hazards, the remedial action must at least ensure that the hazard in the premises ceases to be a Category 1 hazard, but it can require more: section 11(5).

The improvement notice can refer to more than one hazard and category but it cannot require remedial works to start within 28 days of the service of the notice.

Remedial action is action which will remove or reduce the hazard, section11(8). Usually, this takes the form of works to the property. The work proposed needs to be reasonable in relation to the hazard. It can be unreasonable to require work which goes beyond what is necessary to remove a hazard.

The standard of the work must such that it prevents the hazard/s from reoccurring. The remedial work must not be temporary and the local authority officer must properly assess the work/s done to determine this on notification of alleged completion.

An improvement notice can specify alternative schemes of work, leaving the choice of which alternative to adopt to the recipient of the notice: *Wood v Kingston upon Hull City Council [2017] EWCA Civ 364; [2017] H.L.R. 30.* In the case of premises containing flats, remedial action may be required in relation to the common parts or (any part of) the building containing the flats (which may include another flat), but only if the authority are satisfied that the deficiency from which the hazard arises is situated in the common parts of the building, and the action is necessary to protect the health or safety of any actual or potential occupiers of one or more of the flats in it: sections 11(3), (4), 12(3).

Once the work is finished, the improvement notice can be revoked or varied in whole or in part. It might be that financial assistance is required to comply with the notice and in the time given. If this arises the authority ought to consider directing where such assistance can be obtained. This can include such grants as the Disability Facilities Grant, for example.

Should one not comply with the improvement notice, then pursuant to section 31 and Schedule 3 the authority can take the action required by an improvement notice itself, with or without the agreement of the person on whom the notice was served. The need to act with agreement may arise where a category 1 hazard exists and remedial action is required without undue delay, but the owner is not in a position to carry out the works or arrange for the work to be done.

Where the authority acts with the agreement of the person served with the improvement notice the works are to be taken at his or her expense. If the authority takes action without agreement, it may recover expenses reasonably incurred, with interest. If not paid, such expenses may be added as a charge on the property.

If an improvement notice is appealed, it is often on the grounds that someone else ought to pay for the action, that the notice itself and the need for the same is incorrect, or the expenses sought from an authority are disproportionate.

Prohibition Order

A prohibition order under section 20 or 21 is a possible response to a category 1 or a category 2 hazard. It may prohibit the use of part or all of the premises for some or all purposes, or occupation by particular numbers or classes of people.

Pursuant to section 22 the order must state:

a. whether the order is made under section 20 or 21;

b. the nature of the hazard and the premises on which it exists, as well as identifying the cause or deficiency;

c. any remedial action that would result in the order being revoked;

d. the notice must also contain information about the right to appeal.

An order becomes operative 28 days after it is made, unless it is appealed.

Copies of the order must be served on everyone who, to the authority's knowledge, is

an owner, occupier, is authorised to permit occupation, or a mortgage lender in relation

to the whole or part of the premises. Such copies must be served within 7 days of the

making of the order.

In relation to a category 1 hazard, it must be revoked if the authority is satisfied that the hazard no longer exists or if there special circumstances making it appropriate to revoke it.

In relation to a category 2 hazard, it may be revoked where appropriate to do so, including on consideration of an application by one that is served with it.

An appeal can be made by a person served with the order on the grounds that they are the wrong person or the order not being the most appropriate. Such an appeal must be made within 28 days from the date the order was made. It can also be made against a decision on revocation or variation. If the authority refuses to allow the premises to be used for any other purpose while the order is operating, an appeal can also be brought in relation to that refusal within 28 days from the date on which the refusal decision is made.

Generally, such orders can be used to:

a. control the number of people who can occupy a premises with insufficient facilities and/or the type of people who can occupy the premises and for what purpose/s;

b. order remedial action/works without anyone occupying the premises. Sometimes a landlord cannot rehouse the tenant and rarely the authority will assist financially or otherwise to rehouse the tenant.

The authority must consider:

a. what the risks are to the tenant (including temporary decant);

b. whether the building is a listed building and the extent to which the proposed work/s can be carried out;

c. the extent of the proposed works on neighbouring properties and area in which the premises is such as conservation or renewal areas, and in the time frame proposed;

d. the availability of temporary accommodation in the locality to minimise disruption to the tenant;

e. whether any planning permission or licences are required.

Both improvement notices and prohibition orders can be suspended and restart on the event of a trigger occurring as set out in the notice or order. It might be that a more practical, realistic timescale is needing to be factored in and decided upon rather than run the risk of having to suspend it for a time further down the line to allow the landlord the opportunity to source materials, trades etc. With the covid-19 pandemic and Brexit, more leniency as to what timescales are given at the outset is encouraged.

If the notice or order is suspended, it is ill-advised in the event that there is a quick turnover in occupancy.

Suspension is appropriate, however, if, for strategic reasons, it is to ensure that the work/s done are not rushed in an area of renewal. It could be that the work could be done when the property is expected to be vacant such as student accommodation. It is not wise to suspend, however, where there is a category 1 hazard.

Trigger events include a change of occupancy whereby the incoming tenant is more vulnerable and may be more adversely affected by continuing hazards remaining unaddressed for any longer than is necessary.

If there is change of circumstance, it is for the landlord to inform the authority.

Requests to suspend can come from tenants and not just landlords. It might be that the authority takes the view that instead it will issue a hazard awareness notice.

Emergency Options

a. *Emergency Remedial Action*

The authority can take emergency enforcement action against hazards which present an imminent risk of serious harm to occupiers. The authority often takes the remedial action itself and seeks recovery of the expenses from the Landlord.

Providing section 40(1) are fulfilled, an authority may enter the premises at any time to take emergency remedial action to remove the imminent risk of serious harm. It need not be just one hazard that is remedied.

The authority may apply to the magistrates/Justice of the Peace for a warrant to enter the premises to take emergency remedial action. The authority must show that without the warrant it is unlikely to gain admission. There must be reasonable grounds for securing entry.

A notice of emergency remedial action must be served within 7 days of taking that action and must specify:

a. the nature of the hazard and the premises on which it exists, as well as identifying the cause or deficiency;

b. any remedial action which was or is to be taken;

c. the date the action was or is to be started;

d. the notice must also contain information about the right to appeal.

b. Emergency Prohibition Orders

An authority may only make an emergency prohibition order in relation to a Category 1 hazard: section 43(1)(a). The authority must be satisfied that the hazard involves an imminent risk of serious harm to the health and safety of any of the occupiers of the premises concerned, or other residential premises: section 43(1)(b). An emergency order takes immediate effect: section 43(2). The prohibitions on use of the premises are the same as for other prohibition orders. The order must be served on the same persons as a normal prohibition order. It must be served on the day that it is made or, if that is not possible, as soon as possible thereafter: section 43(4).

The order must specify (s.44):

a. the nature of the hazard and the premises on which it exists, as well as identifying the cause or deficiency;

b. any remedial action that would result in the order being revoked;

c. the notice must also contain information about the right to appeal.

The provisions relating to compensation, revocation and variation, and enforcement governing normal orders also apply to emergency orders: section 43(5).

If it is a category 2 hazard, then there is also the option to take emergency remedial action or make an emergency prohibition order.

An emergency prohibition order is served on the day it is made.

A person served with a notice of emergency remedial action can appeal against the action taken, whilst any person who was served with a copy of an emergency prohibition order can appeal against such an order.

Appeals must be made within 28 days of the date emergency remedial action is to be started or the date an emergency prohibition order is made.

c. Interaction with the Rent Act 1977

Where a prohibition order pursuant to section 33 Rent Act 1977 is made in relation to premises let under a regulated tenancy, the effect of such orders is to remove the Rent Act protection. This means that there is a loss of tenure.

This removal of the Rent Act protection enables the landlord to recover possession on the basis that the tenancy has been reduced to a contractual tenancy. The tenancy must still be terminated in the usual way (normally by a notice to quit where the tenancy is periodic), and the landlord will need to obtain a court order for possession.

The Defendant who is evicted in these circumstances may apply to be rehoused by the local authority under the Land Compensation Act 1973, section 39(1).

The authority has a duty to secure that the former tenant will be provided with suitable alternative residential accommodation on reasonable terms.

A displaced tenant will also be entitled to claim a home loss payment from the authority pursuant to the Rent Act 1977, section 29.

A landlord can only obtain possession in cases of rent act tenants, for example, by establishing one of the grounds set out in s.98 and Schedule 15 to the Act.

A protected tenancy must come to an end in one of the ways prescribed at common law. The same rules apply to protected tenancies as other tenancies. Once the protected/contractual tenancy has been determined, however, then if and so long as the tenant occupies the dwelling-house as his residence he shall be a statutory tenant, section 2(1) of the Rent Act 1977.

The tenancy must have been protected immediately before it was determined – s.2(1)(a), *Stagg v Brickett [1951] 1 K.B. 648.*

The tenant must substantially use the premises as his residence, however – see, for example *Skinner v Geary [1931] 2 K.B. 546.* The occupation as a residence must be continual in order for the statutory tenancy to arise and to continue, *John M Brown Ltd v Bestwick [1951] 1 K.B. 21.*

Unlike the Housing Act 1988, the tenant need not occupy the premises as his only or principal residence. This means that a tenant can occupy more than one property as his home – *Langford Property Co v Tureman [1949] 1 K.B. 29.* Both premises must, however, be used as a home in order to obtain protection, and not merely be a place used when convenience and rarely – *Zetie v Cohen (1958) 172 E.G. 371.*

Unfortunately, this means that because the property is not 'habitable' (prohibition order) it cannot be used as a 'home' whilst works are ongoing. It cannot be possible to state it is 'occupied' in order to satisfy the requirement of 'living there'.

Section 98(1)(a) provides that the court may make an order for possession if the court is satisfied that suitable alternative accommodation is available for the tenant or will be available for him when the order in question takes effect. The burden of showing that suitable alternative accommodation is (or will be) available is on the landlord (*Nevile v Hardy [1921] 1 Ch. 404*) although if it raises a prima facie case the burden will shift to the tenant (*Mason v Murray [1946] E.G.D. 208*).

The discretionary grounds (other than suitable alternative accommodation) are set out in Pt 1 of Sch.15 Housing Act 2004. If a Landlord were unsuccessful under section 33 Housing Act 2004, they may attempt to rely on Case 3, 'deterioration in the condition of the dwelling-house'.

In relation to discretionary grounds the court may only make an order if it considers it reasonable to do so and either:

a. Suitable alternative accommodation is available (or will be when the order for possession takes effect); or

b. Ground under Pt 1 of Sch.15 is satisfied.

There are two ways of establishing suitable alternative accommodation provided for by Pt IV of Sch.15.

The first is to obtain a local authority certificate that it will provide suitable alternative accommodation – para.3 of Pt IV of Sch.15. This is very unlikely to happen in practice, however.

The second is for the landlord to prove suitable alternative accommodation is, or will be, available by satisfying certain requirements:

a. The first requirement relates to security of tenure. The alternative accommodation must be let under a protected tenancy or some other type of tenancy which provides reasonably equivalent security of tenure. I do not consider a licence or AST to provide sufficient protection.

b. The second requirements relates to the premises themselves. The conditions which must be satisfied are that the accommodation is:

> *"reasonably suitable to the needs of the tenant and his family as regards proximity to place of work, and either-*
>
> *(a) similar as regards rental and extent to the accommodation afforded by dwelling-houses provided in the neighbourhood by any housing authority for persons whose needs as regards extent are, in the opinion of the court, similar to those of the tenant and of his family; or*
>
> *(b) reasonably suitable to the means of the tenant and to the needs of the tenant and his family as regards extent and character; and that if any furniture was provided for use under the protected or statutory tenancy in question, furniture is provided for use in the accommodation which is either similar to that so provided or is reasonably suitable to the needs of the tenant and his family."*

If a tenant stands to lose their security of tenure if such an order is served, they likely will have good grounds for appealing under section 45 of the Housing Act 200.4 to the F-tT. The landlord may be called upon to evidence how it can establish alternative accommodation. The authority is likely to be called upon to explain why what is sought to be achieved cannot be done with the rent act tenant in situ.

Hazard Awareness Notice

A hazard awareness notice under section 29 may be use in response to a less serious hazard, where the authority wishes to draw attention to the desirability of remedial action.

Pursuant to section 28 it can also be used in response to a category 1 hazard as long as no management order is in place under Part 4. There may be circumstances where works of improvement, or prohibition of the use of the whole or part of the premises, are not practicable or reasonable, and, as set out above, it is considered that a hazard awareness notice is more appropriate.

It must specify:

a. the nature of the hazard and the premises on which it exists, as well as identifying the cause or deficiency;

b. any remedial action that the authority considers appropriate and practicable to take;

c. reasons for the notice and why this course of action has been chosen;

d. the notice must also contain information about the right to appeal.

No further action is required by the person served with the notice but the purpose of it is to encourage work/s to be carried out so that the notice, and hazards, do not escalate or morph into a different notice or course of action.

One cannot appeal against a hazard awareness notice and there is no requirement to register these notices as a local land charge. They are, at their core, advisory notices. It is for the authority to keep track of what has been served and on who.

Such a notice may be used where the landlord or owner has agreed to take remedial action

and the authority is confident the work will be done in reasonable time.

Demolition orders

Pursuant to Part 9 of the 1985 Act, such orders can be used in response to a category 1 hazard unless the premises are a listed building.

Relevant factors to consider include the demand for accommodation in which the hazard was found, the use of the cleared site, current housing stock and availability of local accommodation for rehousing.

The order must be served on every person authorise to permit occupation or is a mortgage lender in relation to the whole pr part of the premises within 7 days from the date the order is made.

One may appeal within 21 days of service of the order.

Clearance Areas

Pursuant to Part 9 of the 1985 Act, an authority can declare an area a clearance area if it is satisfied that each of the residential buildings in the area contains one or more category 1 hazards (or that these buildings are dangerous or harmful to the health or safety of the inhabitants); and any other buildings in the area are dangerous or harmful to the health of the inhabitants. In a building containing flats, two or more of those flats must contain a category 1 hazard before a clearance area can be declared.

Factors to consider include:

a. long-term demand for residential accommodation;

b. density of the buildings and street pattern;

c. narrowness of the buildings;

d. whether land can be acquired around the proposed clearance area and with who would an agreement be required;

e. any protected buildings;

f. other rights such as existing rights to telecommunication companies to have a mast or similar on a building;

g. proposed after-use and socio-economic impact;

h. the practicalities of rehousing displaced occupants.

Other Options to the Housing Act 2004

Injunction

If the local authority would rather have access to other remedies such an injunction or wider means of enforcement, then proceedings can be brought in the High Court. If the local authority is of the view that the criminal proceedings are inadequate, then the power to reach that opinion must be properly delegated. It can be reached by a committee sub-committee or officer of the council, but not be made by a single member (*R v Secretary of State for the Environment, ex p London Borough of Hillingdon [1986] 1 WLR 192*. The decision ought not be made before a claim is issued or soon afterwards. Delegation, on the other hand, cannot be done retrospectively (see *Bowyer, Philpott and Payne Ltd v Mather [1919] 1 KB 419*).

Should an injunction be sought such a remedy cannot be obtained under section 81(5) unless an abatement notice has first been served under section 80(1).

Criminal proceedings cannot be considered inadequate merely because they are not as convenient, see *Vale of White Horse District Council v Allen & Partners [1997] Env LR 212*. In *City of Bradford Metropolitan Council v Brown and others [1987] 19 HLR 16*, the Court of Appeal considered the preceding legislation containing the same power as under section 81(5) of the EPA 1990. It cautioned that even though the court has jurisdiction to grant an injunction to restrain a breach of the criminal law, it will normally only do so where there has been a complete disregard for the statutory prohibition. Practitioners ought to tread carefully and exercise reluctance when dealing with hoarders because they probably do not appreciate the danger/s of what they are doing and/or the nuisance they are causing, even if this is explained to them. A court is also likely to be reluctant to grant an injunction which makes a defendant liable to a penalty which is much greater than the penalty imposed for the offence.

When considering such an application for injunction, therefore the local authority should carefully consider the impact it could have on one's human rights. A failure to do so could be a bar to the granting of the injunction. The EHCR will play a part in the discretion to be exercised by the judge as to whether and in what terms to grant an injunctive remedy.

Plainly, the Public Sector Equality Duty pursuant to section 149 will apply (see further below).

Section 149(1) sets out the public sector equality duty ('PSED'), which requires that a public authority:

> "*must, in the exercise of its functions, have due regard to the need to: (a) eliminate discrimination, harassment, victimisation and any other conduct that is prohibited by or under this Act; (b) advance equality of opportunity between persons who share a relevant protected characteristic and persons who do not share it.*"

Section 149(3) provides that:

> "*having due regard to the need to advance equality of opportunity between persons who share a relevant protected characteristic and persons who do not share it involves having due regard, in particular, to the need to: (a) remove or minimise disadvantages suffered by persons who share a relevant protected characteristic that are connected*

> *to that characteristic [and] (b) take steps to meet the needs of persons who share a relevant protected characteristic that are different from the needs of persons who do not share it.....".*

Section 149(4) provides that

> *"the steps involved in meeting the needs of disabled persons that are different from the needs of persons who are not disabled include, in particular, steps to take account of disabled persons' disabilities."*

Further, section 149(6) recognises that

> *"compliance with the duties in this section may involve treating some persons more favourably than others; but that is not to be taken as permitting conduct that would otherwise be prohibited by or under this Act".*

It is likely to be rare that a person will be aggrieved with a local authority for failing to inspect a property rather than its failure to investigate his or her particular complaint of a statutory nuisance. If there is evidence of the absence of a scheme of inspection, on the other hand, this is likely to support the view that the local authority has not properly discharged the PSED.

A local authority is unlikely to be able to plead successfully that lack of resources is the reason for its failure to discharge the PSED properly. It should take into account the question of finances in deciding what method of inspection it should employ (and enforcement), see *R v Gloucestershire County Council, ex p Barry [1997] AC 584*. If the result of considering the financial consequences is to employ a method of action or enforcement that is not as effective than if the local authority spent greater money on the matter, then community groups and individuals could call to question the methodology and decision making adopted. Assessing how it will carry out its duty and allocate resources for inspection of an area or property and its connection to the PSED is arguable following *R (Harris) v Haringey LBC [2010] EWCA Civ 703.*

When considering an injunction, the local authority is no longer necessarily having to consider the principles of *Shelfer v City of London Electric Lighting Co [1895] 1 Ch 287:*

a. If the injury to the applicant's legal right is small;

b. Is it one which is capable of being estimate in money;

c. Is it one which can be compensated by money;

d. Is the injunction sought oppressive.

The case of *Coventry and others v Lawrence and Others [2014] UKSC 13* confirmed that a more flexible approach than the *Shelfer* test can be considered.

Building Act 1984

a. Section 76 – 'dangerous structure' and 'defective building'

Sometimes the enforcement procedures aforesaid is not sufficiently quick or insufficient within themselves to address what is a 'prejudice to health'. For urgent cases there are emergency procedures set out in section 76 of the Building Act 1984 that can be considered.

This enables the local authority to deal with dangerous buildings that have may have become dangerous causing joists and flooring to give way and/or cause the property to subside.

The term 'dangerous structure' means any building, part of a building o other structure where it poses a serious danger to the public.

A 'defective building' does not pose a serious danger but will have an impact on the visual amenity of an area, and the welfare of the public therein.

b. Section 77 – procedure

Pursuant to section 77, the local authority may apply to the magistrates' court if the building is dangerous. The court may:

a. Where the danger arises from the condition of the building or structure – make an order requiring the owner to:

   i. Execute such work/s as may be necessary to obviate the danger; or

   ii. Demolish the building or structure, or any dangerous part of it, and remove any rubbish resulting from the demolition.

b. Where the danger arises from overloading, the local authority can request an order restricting its use until the court withdraws or modifies the restriction.

Should one not comply upon service of the order, then the local authority may:

a. Execute the order, and

b. Recover the expenses reasonably incurred by it in doing so form the person at fault.

Criminally, the person may also be liable to pay a fine not exceeding level 1 on the standard scale.

c. Section 78 – emergency measures

Pursuant to section 78, there are emergency measures available where:

a. If the building or part of a building or structure is in such a state or is used to carry such loads as to be dangerous; and

b. Immediate action should be taken to remove the danger, then the local authority nay take necessary steps.

The local authority can recover the costs reasonably incurred pursuant to sections 78(3)-(6). The court has the discretion to:

a. Not award expenses if the local authority could have used powers under section 77 instead;

b. Decide whether some of the expenses should be paid by another person

c. Make an order proportionate to the court.

Owners may claim compensation for any damage incurred as a result of the local authority's action/s if the owner or occupier can show there has been no default of any obligations under the Building Act 1984.

Prevention of Damage by Pests Act 1949

Section 4 of the Prevention of Damage by Pests Act 1949 ('PDPA 1949') gives local authorities the power to require an owner or occupier of a property to act to prevent or treat an infestation of rats or mice. The owner or occupier of the property should be served with a notice setting out reasonable steps to destroy the rats or mice within a reasonable period. Steps could include removing materials from land or premises, carrying out structural work or carrying out pest control treatment.

Where there is a failure to carry out the steps specified, the relevant local authority may carry these out and recover the costs from the notice recipient (section 5).

It should be noted that there is no specific power of entry under section 5 of the PDPA 1949. Therefore, a local authority will not be able to carry out the necessary works if they are denied access. Where the owner of the land is not the occupier, separate notices may be served on both. If the occupier of the property prevents the owner carrying out the required works, the court may order the occupier to permit the work to be carried out.

This power is generally exercised by local authorities in relation to the clearing of gardens and external spaces rather than for internal clearance (where the Public Health Act 1936 powers tend to be used, see Housing Act 2004 (HHSRS)).

Clean Neighbourhoods and Environment Act 2005 ('the 2005 Act')

This provides local authorities with powers to tackle poor environmental quality and anti-social behaviour, including amendments to the Refuse Disposal (Amenity) Act 1978. It includes sections on nuisance and abandoned vehicles, litter, graffiti, waste, noise and dogs.

Refuse Disposal (Amenity) Act 1978

This piece of legislation is likely to be relied on by local authorities where the hazard is visible and affecting the amenity of an area, however, it does require the relevant owner to have abandoned.

Abandoned Vehicles

This Act is generally used in cases of abandoned vehicle/s, which may be the chosen item of a hoarder to accumulate. Section 2 places a duty on local authorities to remove motor vehicles abandoned on land in the open air and can recover its costs from either the owner or the person who abandoned it.

Section 2A (as inserted by the Clean Neighbourhoods and Environment Act 2005) gives an authorised officer the power to issue a fixed penalty notice in respect of an offence of abandoning a vehicle. Section 2B enables an authorised officer to require the name and address of the person to whom he proposes to issue a fixed penalty notice and section 2C enables local authorities to use the receipts from these penalties for the purposes of their functions under the 1978 Act and sections 99 to 102 of the Road Traffic Regulation Act 1984.

No notice is required to be given by the local authority where a vehicle is abandoned on a road. Once the authority is satisfied the vehicle has been abandoned it can be removed immediately. Section 11 of the 2005 Act amends section 3 of the 1978 Act. Section 11(2) removes the requirement to serve a notice on the occupier of land where the vehicle is on a 'road'. The 2005 Act enables local authorities to immediately remove any vehicle in such a condition that it thinks it has been abandoned. The fixed penalty notice amount is £200.

Abandoned vehicles should not be confused with untaxed vehicles. Untaxed vehicles are not classed as abandoned. It is the responsibility, in that event, for the DVLA to remove, If the vehicle/s is causing an obstruction then it can be removed and dealt with by the police pursuant to relevant traffic regulations and police powers. Untaxed vehicles on private land can be removed if it is not SORN and/or is not on the property/land with permission. This includes removal from secure car parks and/or public car parks.

Nuisance parking

These offences are aimed at businesses that use the public road as a 'showroom' and people who use the road as a 'workshop'. The latter is more likely with hoarders.

Of most relevance is section 4 of the 2005 Act whereby it is an offence to carry out 'restricted works' to vehicles on a road. 'Restricted Works' covers repair, maintenance, servicing, improving or the dismantling of a motor vehicle or any part or accessory. The maximum fine is level 4 on the standard scale on summary conviction. The power to issue a fixed penalty notice is found at section 6 and the amount is £100.

Public Health Act 1961

Section 34 of the Public Health Act 1961 empowers a local authority to remove accumulations of rubbish that are seriously detrimental to the amenity of a neighbourhood, such as the garden of a hoarder's property.

'Rubbish' includes rubble, waste paper, crockery, metal and any other kind of refuse (including organic matter).

A notice should be served on the relevant owner and occupier of the land at least 28 days before any action is taken outlining the proposed steps to be taken and reliance on section 34. The notice recipient and any other person with an interest in the land may, within 28 days of being served the notice, either:

a. Serve a counter notice stating that they will take those steps;

b. Appeal to the magistrates' court on the grounds that the local authority was not justified in taking action or the steps proposed were unreasonable.

There is also a power under section 36 of the Public Health Act 1961 to require the vacation of the affected premises while fumigation is being undertaken to destroy any vermin. This power could be used by a local authority in conjunction with section 83 of the Public Health Act 1936. Where this is required by a local authority, it must provide alternative shelter or accommodation free of charge for the relevant individual until the fumigation is complete.

Public Health Act 1936

There are several provisions in the Public Health Act 1936 ('PHA 1936').

Pursuant to section 79, a local authority has the power to require removal of noxious matter by occupiers of premises in an urban district if it appears to the proper officer of the authority that the accumulation of such matter ought to be removed. Under this section, a local authority may recover the expenses of any action taken from the relevant owner or occupier in default. This provision is not generally relied on by authorities as more recent legislation exists which is more appropriate.

Section 83 requires the cleansing of any premises which are in a *"filthy or unwholesome condition as to be prejudicial to health or are verminous"*.

Under this provision, a notice should be served on the owner or occupier of the premises requiring certain steps to be taken within a stated period (generally a minimum of 21 days) to remedy their condition (this may require the removal of wall coverings or the destruction or removal of any vermin). A failure to comply with a notice under section 83 will allow a local authority to undertake the works itself and to recover the costs from the owner. There is no appeal against the issue of such a notice.

Section 84 gives local authorities a power to cleanse, purify, disinfect or destroy any filthy or verminous articles found in a property at their own expense.

CHAPTER EIGHT

RENT REPAYMENT ORDERS

What are they and what is the purpose?

Rent repayment orders are a means by which a tenant or local authority can seek to have up to 12 months of rent, housing benefit or universal credit repaid.

The Housing Act 2004 introduced rent repayment orders to cover situations where the landlord of a property had failed to obtain a licence for a property that was required to be licensed, specifically offences in relation to licensing of Houses in Multiple Occupation (section 72(1)) and offences in relation to licensing of houses under Part 3 of the Act (section 95(1)).

The Housing & Planning Act 2016 introduced a range of measures to crack down on rogue landlords.

When extended rent repayment orders were introduced through the Housing and Planning Act 2016, Ministers made clear that they expected this power to be used robustly as a way of clamping down on rogue landlords. In the House of Commons, Brandon Lewis MP (then Minister of State for Housing and Planning at the Department for Communities and Local Government) made the following statement on 8 February 2016:

> *"[This] will enable councils to issue remedy payment orders for up to 12 months. That will give them a resource that [it is hoped] they will use"*

Who can apply and make the order and what are the restrictions?

Local Authorities

The First-tier Tribunal will only consider making an order for a local authority if the offence falls within the local authority's boundaries, and the landlord has already received a 'notice intending proceedings' setting out that they have not less than 28 days within which he or she is to make representations for consideration.

If this notice period has not expired then the local authority may not apply for the rent repayment order.

Tenants

They may apply directly to the First-tier Tribunal for a rent repayment order. The tenant must have lived in the property within the preceding 12 months and the offence must have happened in that time.

What are the offences?

Rent repayment orders were extended to cover the following situations:

a. Failure to comply with an Improvement Notice under section 30 of the Housing Act 2004;

b. Failure to comply with a Prohibition Order under section 32 of the Housing Act 2004;

c. Breach of a banning order made under section 21 of the Housing and Planning Act 2016;

d. Using violence to secure entry to a property under section 6 of the Criminal Law Act 1977; and

e. Illegal eviction or harassment of the occupiers of a property under section 1 of the Protection from Eviction Act 1977.

How is it calculated?

The First-tier Tribunal must order that the maximum amount of rent (up to 12 months) is repaid where the landlord has been convicted of the offence to which the rent repayment order applies. This is regardless of whether or not the local housing authority or tenant has applied for a lesser amount. Where the landlord has not been convicted, the First-tier Tribunal will determine the amount to be repaid in accordance with section 44 (tenants) or section 45 (local housing authorities) of the Housing and Planning Act 2016. Regard may be had for the severity of the breach/offence of, for example, the improvement notice, and whether access has been problematic at any time to comply with the said notice or order.

Where a landlord has been convicted of any of the offences listed above and the rent repayment order, or part of it, is being made in favour of the local housing authority (because rent was paid through Housing Benefit/Universal Credit), the First-tier Tribunal must require the landlord to repay all of the rent paid to the landlord by the local housing authority up to a maximum of 12 months, provided the conditions in section 46 of the Housing and Planning Act 2016 are met.

The amount to be repaid to the local housing authority will be determined in accordance with section 45 of the Housing and Planning Act 2016 while for the tenant, the amount to be repaid will be determined in accordance with section 44 of the Act.

The following formula should be used to calculate the amount of rent that should be repaid to the tenant and the amount paid to the local housing authority where the tenant is in receipt of benefits:

$x = (a / c) * d$

$y = x - b$

where:

a = rent liability

b = rent allowance

c = maximum Universal Credit award

d = net Universal Credit award

x = amount to be retained by local housing authority

y = amount to be paid to tenant

How to apply?

A tenant only needs to submit a claim to the First-tier Tribunal which sets out the reasons for the claim and the dates to which it relates.

A 'notice intending proceedings' must be served on the landlord if brought by the local authority.

Where a landlord has been convicted of the offence to which the rent repayment order relates, the First-tier Tribunal must order that the maximum amount of rent is repaid (capped at a maximum of 12 months).

A rent repayment order can be applied for when the landed has committed an offence whether or not the landlord has been convicted of the offences detailed aforesaid.

In the absence of a conviction, the First-tier Tribunal needs to be satisfied beyond all reasonable doubt that the landlord has committed the offence.

Even if there is a conviction, a rent repayment order is not automatically awarded in respect of the relevant offence.

Other things to consider

A landlord may appeal against a decision of the First-tier Tribunal to the Upper Tribunal provided that permission to appeal has been given by the First-tier Tribunal or the Upper Tribunal.

Where the landlord fails to pay a rent repayment order, the local housing authority or tenant should refer the case to the county court for an Order of that Court.

A local housing authority can impose a civil penalty and apply for a rent repayment order where there is failure to comply with an improvement notice under section 30.

The rent repayment order power only applies to those parts of the property being rented out to a tenant. Common parts are not included and such orders can only be applied for against the landlord, not a managing agent or head tenant.

MORE BOOKS BY LAW BRIEF PUBLISHING

A selection of our other titles available now:-

'A Practical Guide to Transgender Law' by Robin Moira White & Nicola Newbegin
'Artificial Intelligence – The Practical Legal Issues (2nd Edition)' by John Buyers
'A Practical Guide to Challenging Sham Marriage Allegations in Immigration Law' by Priya Solanki
'A Practical Guide to New Build Conveyancing' by Paul Sams & Rebecca East
'A Practical Guide to Inherited Wealth on Divorce' by Hayley Trim
'A Practical Guide to Shareholder Disputes in Family Businesses' by Ed Weeks
'A Practical Guide to the Law of Forests in Scotland' by Philip Buchan
'A Practical Guide to Health and Medical Cases in Immigration Law' by Rebecca Chapman & Miranda Butler
'A Practical Guide to Bad Character Evidence for Criminal Practitioners by Aparna Rao
'A Practical Guide to Environmental Enforcement' by Christopher Badger & Stuart Jessop
'A Practical Guide to Hoarding and Mental Health for Housing Lawyers' by Rachel Coyle
'A Practical Guide to Psychiatric Claims in Personal Injury – 2nd Edition' by Liam Ryan
'Stephens on Contractual Indemnities' by Richard Stephens
'A Practical Guide to the EU Succession Regulation' by Richard Frimston
'A Practical Guide to Solicitor and Client Costs – 2nd Edition' by Robin Dunne
'Constructive Dismissal – Practice Pointers and Principles' by Benjimin Burgher
'A Practical Guide to Religion and Belief Discrimination Claims in the Workplace' by Kashif Ali
'A Practical Guide to the Law of Medical Treatment Decisions' by Ben Troke

'Fundamental Dishonesty and QOCS in Personal Injury Proceedings: Law and Practice' by Jake Rowley
'A Practical Guide to the Law in Relation to School Exclusions' by Charlotte Hadfield & Alice de Coverley
'A Practical Guide to Divorce for the Silver Separators' by Karin Walker
'The Right to be Forgotten – The Law and Practical Issues' by Melissa Stock
'A Practical Guide to Planning Law and Rights of Way in National Parks, the Broads and AONBs' by James Maurici QC, James Neill et al
'A Practical Guide to Election Law' by Tom Tabori
'A Practical Guide to the Law in Relation to Surrogacy' by Andrew Powell
'A Practical Guide to Claims Arising from Fatal Accidents – 2nd Edition' by James Patience
'A Practical Guide to the Ownership of Employee Inventions – From Entitlement to Compensation' by James Tumbridge & Ashley Roughton
'A Practical Guide to Asbestos Claims' by Jonathan Owen & Gareth McAloon
'A Practical Guide to Stamp Duty Land Tax in England and Northern Ireland' by Suzanne O'Hara
'A Practical Guide to the Law of Farming Partnerships' by Philip Whitcomb
'Covid-19, Homeworking and the Law – The Essential Guide to Employment and GDPR Issues' by Forbes Solicitors
'Covid-19, Force Majeure and Frustration of Contracts – The Essential Guide' by Keith Markham
'Covid-19 and Criminal Law – The Essential Guide' by Ramya Nagesh
'Covid-19 and Family Law in England and Wales – The Essential Guide' by Safda Mahmood
'A Practical Guide to the Law of Unlawful Eviction and Harassment – 2nd Edition' by Stephanie Lovegrove
'Covid-19, Residential Property, Equity Release and Enfranchisement – The Essential Guide' by Paul Sams and Louise Uphill
'Covid-19, Brexit and the Law of Commercial Leases – The Essential Guide' by Mark Shelton
'A Practical Guide to Costs in Personal Injury Claims – 2nd Edition' by Matthew Hoe

'A Practical Guide to the General Data Protection Regulation (GDPR) – 2nd Edition' by Keith Markham
'Ellis on Credit Hire – Sixth Edition' by Aidan Ellis & Tim Kevan
'A Practical Guide to Working with Litigants in Person and McKenzie Friends in Family Cases' by Stuart Barlow
'Protecting Unregistered Brands: A Practical Guide to the Law of Passing Off' by Lorna Brazell
'A Practical Guide to Secondary Liability and Joint Enterprise Post-Jogee' by Joanne Cecil & James Mehigan
'A Practical Guide to the Pre-Action RTA Claims Protocol for Personal Injury Lawyers' by Antonia Ford
'A Practical Guide to Neighbour Disputes and the Law' by Alexander Walsh
'A Practical Guide to Forfeiture of Leases' by Mark Shelton
'A Practical Guide to Coercive Control for Legal Practitioners and Victims' by Rachel Horman
'A Practical Guide to Rights Over Airspace and Subsoil' by Daniel Gatty
'Tackling Disclosure in the Criminal Courts – A Practitioner's Guide' by Narita Bahra QC & Don Ramble
'A Practical Guide to the Law of Driverless Cars – Second Edition' by Alex Glassbrook, Emma Northey & Scarlett Milligan
'A Practical Guide to TOLATA Claims' by Greg Williams
'A Practical Guide to Elderly Law – 2nd Edition' by Justin Patten
'A Practical Guide to the Law of Prescription in Scotland' by Andrew Foyle
'A Practical Guide to the Construction and Rectification of Wills and Trust Instruments' by Edward Hewitt
'A Practical Guide to the Law of Bullying and Harassment in the Workplace' by Philip Hyland
'How to Be a Freelance Solicitor: A Practical Guide to the SRA-Regulated Freelance Solicitor Model' by Paul Bennett
'A Practical Guide to Prison Injury Claims' by Malcolm Johnson
'A Practical Guide to the Small Claims Track - 2nd Edition' by Dominic Bright
'A Practical Guide to Advising Clients at the Police Station' by Colin Stephen McKeown-Beaumont

‘A Practical Guide to Antisocial Behaviour Injunctions’ by Iain Wightwick

‘Practical Mediation: A Guide for Mediators, Advocates, Advisers, Lawyers, and Students in Civil, Commercial, Business, Property, Workplace, and Employment Cases’ by Jonathan Dingle with John Sephton

‘The Mini-Pupillage Workbook’ by David Boyle

‘A Practical Guide to Crofting Law’ by Brian Inkster

‘A Practical Guide to Spousal Maintenance’ by Liz Cowell

‘A Practical Guide to the Law of Domain Names and Cybersquatting’ by Andrew Clemson

‘A Practical Guide to the Law of Gender Pay Gap Reporting’ by Harini Iyengar

‘A Practical Guide to the Rights of Grandparents in Children Proceedings’ by Stuart Barlow

‘NHS Whistleblowing and the Law’ by Joseph England

‘Employment Law and the Gig Economy’ by Nigel Mackay & Annie Powell

‘A Practical Guide to Noise Induced Hearing Loss (NIHL) Claims’ by Andrew Mckie, Ian Skeate, Gareth McAloon

‘An Introduction to Beauty Negligence Claims – A Practical Guide for the Personal Injury Practitioner’ by Greg Almond

‘Intercompany Agreements for Transfer Pricing Compliance’ by Paul Sutton

‘Zen and the Art of Mediation’ by Martin Plowman

‘A Practical Guide to the SRA Principles, Individual and Law Firm Codes of Conduct 2019 – What Every Law Firm Needs to Know’ by Paul Bennett

‘A Practical Guide to Adoption for Family Lawyers’ by Graham Pegg

‘A Practical Guide to Industrial Disease Claims’ by Andrew Mckie & Ian Skeate

‘A Practical Guide to Redundancy’ by Philip Hyland

‘A Practical Guide to Vicarious Liability’ by Mariel Irvine

‘A Practical Guide to Applications for Landlord’s Consent and Variation of Leases’ by Mark Shelton

‘A Practical Guide to Relief from Sanctions Post-Mitchell and Denton’ by Peter Causton

‘A Practical Guide to Equity Release for Advisors’ by Paul Sams

‘A Practical Guide to Financial Services Claims’ by Chris Hegarty

'The Law of Houses in Multiple Occupation: A Practical Guide to HMO Proceedings' by Julian Hunt
'Occupiers, Highways and Defective Premises Claims: A Practical Guide Post-Jackson – 2nd Edition' by Andrew Mckie
'A Practical Guide to Financial Ombudsman Service Claims' by Adam Temple & Robert Scrivenor
'A Practical Guide to Advising Schools on Employment Law' by Jonathan Holden
'A Practical Guide to Running Housing Disrepair and Cavity Wall Claims: 2nd Edition' by Andrew Mckie & Ian Skeate
'A Practical Guide to Holiday Sickness Claims – 2nd Edition' by Andrew Mckie & Ian Skeate
'Arguments and Tactics for Personal Injury and Clinical Negligence Claims' by Dorian Williams
'A Practical Guide to Drone Law' by Rufus Ballaster, Andrew Firman, Eleanor Clot
'A Practical Guide to Compliance for Personal Injury Firms Working With Claims Management Companies' by Paul Bennett
'RTA Allegations of Fraud in a Post-Jackson Era: The Handbook – 2nd Edition' by Andrew Mckie
'RTA Personal Injury Claims: A Practical Guide Post-Jackson' by Andrew Mckie
'On Experts: CPR35 for Lawyers and Experts' by David Boyle
'An Introduction to Personal Injury Law' by David Boyle
'A Practical Guide to Subtle Brain Injury Claims' by Pankaj Madan

These books and more are available to order online direct from the publisher at www.lawbriefpublishing.com, where you can also read free sample chapters. For any queries, contact us on 0844 587 2383 or mail@lawbriefpublishing.com.

Our books are also usually in stock at www.amazon.co.uk with free next day delivery for Prime members, and at good legal bookshops such as Wildy & Sons.

We are regularly launching new books in our series of practical day-to-day practitioners' guides. Visit our website and join our free newsletter to be kept informed and to receive special offers, free chapters, etc.

You can also follow us on Twitter at www.twitter.com/lawbriefpub.

www.ingramcontent.com/pod-product-compliance
Lightning Source LLC
LaVergne TN
LVHW022102200926
848481LV00003B/1044